Sunset Travel Guide to
WESTERN CANADA

By the Editors of Sunset Books and Sunset Magazine

Special Consultant: Mimi Bell

Lane Books · Menlo Park, California

Acknowledgments

We wish to acknowledge with appreciation the excellent cooperation that we received from Canadian officials in supplying and checking information for this book. We would like to thank specifically the following persons who worked closely with us:

JAMES BENSLEY, Director, Greater Vancouver Visitors and Convention Bureau.

JOHN BUCKLEY, Assistant Executive Director, British Columbia Department of Travel Industry.

ELIZABETH BYRD, Grouse Mountain Resorts Ltd., Vancouver.

A. H. CLOUGH, Supervisor, Visitor Services, City of Edmonton.

RODNEY FRASER, Director, San Francisco Office, British Columbia Department of Travel Industry.

FRANK J. HUTTON, Publicity Officer, City of Edmonton.

DOUG JOHNSON, Executive Vice-President, Calgary Tourist and Convention Association.

J. C. K. MADSEN, Associate Director, Banff School of Fine Arts.

WYN McINTYRE, Travel Information Officer, Alberta Government Travel Bureau.

H. P. McKEEVER, Director of Publicity, British Columbia Department of Travel Industry.

G. ED MEADE, Supervisor, British Columbia Travel Bureau.

H. J. MERILEES, M.L.A., Vancouver-Burrard, Director of Fund Raising, Greater Vancouver Visitors and Convention Bureau.

DAVID MOILLIET, Manager, San Francisco Office, Canadian Government Travel Bureau.

MICHAEL S. OVENELL, Regional Co-ordinator, Greater Vancouver Visitors and Convention Bureau.

BUD PAULS, Staff Press Officer, British Columbia Department of Recreation and Conservation.

GEORGE W. POWELL, European General Manager, Canadian Government Travel Bureau.

FRANK SMITH, Manager, Travel and Convention Association of Southern Alberta.

DAN WALLACE, Director, Canadian Government Travel Bureau.

MRS. MELBA WOELFLE, Head, Editorial Services, Canadian Government Travel Bureau.

ILLUSTRATIONS by Dinah James
COVER: Maligne Lake, Jasper National Park.
Photograph by George Hunter.

First Printing April 1970

All rights reserved throughout the world. First Edition. Copyright © 1970 by Lane Magazine & Book Company, Menlo Park, California. Library of Congress No. 74-100902. SBN Title No. 376-06931-6. Lithographed in U.S.A.

CONTENTS

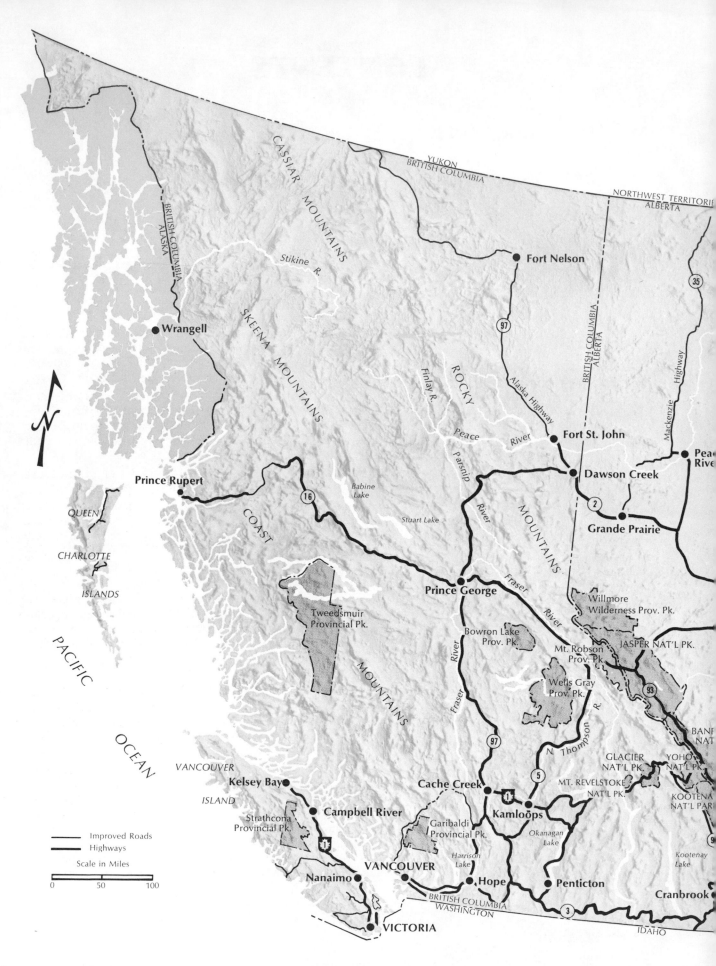

INTRODUCTION:

WESTERN CANADA

Canada's westernmost provinces—British Columbia and Alberta—reach northward from the 49th parallel, bordering the states of Washington, Idaho, and Montana, to the 60th parallel, touching the provinces of the Yukon and Northwest Territories.

From its deeply notched coast, British Columbia stretches eastward across mountains, grassland plateaus, and the great Rocky Mountain Trench (source of the mighty Columbia River), and up the western slopes of the Rocky Mountains, which separate the two provinces.

On the other side of the Rockies, broad plains extend eastward from the foothills across Alberta, Saskatchewan, and Manitoba.

Western Canada is a vast and varied land. It encompasses progressive cities, spectacular scenery, abundant wildlife, and some of Canada's finest farming land. Here, too, is Canada's oil capital; strict regulations minimize the visible evidence of the extensive oil and gas resources below the surface.

The spirit and vigor of the frontier still lingers. Today's roads follow the trails blazed several centuries ago by Indian tribes, explorers, fur traders, and gold seekers. Totem poles are reminders of the Indian heritage. Reconstructed forts recall the years when members of the North-West Mounted Police patrolled to keep order. Annual celebrations enthusiastically revive the days of the cattle era and gold rush.

Long before man arrived, prehistoric animals roamed this land. Millions of years ago, a semi-tropical inland sea covered part of what is now Alberta, and scientists have discovered fossilized remains of dinosaurs, sabertooth cats, three-toed horses, and camels, as well as of such plants as yucca, ginkgo, and palm trees.

Western Canada is sportsmen's country. Hunters are drawn by trophy-size moose and bear, as well as by caribou, elk, deer, mountain sheep and goats. Feisty salmon, steelhead, and Kamloops trout attract fishermen. Sailors cruise the protected waters between Vancouver Island and the mainland, while secluded lakes attract canoeists. Skiers and mountaineers find ample challenge, and golfers have many courses from which to choose. In the cities, spectators can enjoy football, hockey, lacrosse, or horse racing; cricket and

FISHERMAN'S COVE on Howe Sound, north of Vancouver, is a favorite harbor for sailors. Dozens of small boats are moored here.

KLONDIKE MIKE welcomes visitors to Edmonton's Klondike Days.

lawn bowling, curling and ice skating—depending on the season—are also to be found.

Nine of Canada's 19 national parks are in Western Canada; four of them are in British Columbia, five are in Alberta. The Continental Divide, which marks the boundary between the provinces, also divides several adjoining parks.

Canada claims one-third of the world's fresh water; much of it flows from Western Canada's snowfields. Great rivers like the Fraser, the Thompson, and the Columbia eventually find the Pacific Ocean. The Saskatchewan, the Peace, and the Athabasca go the other direction, emptying into Arctic waters. Others, like the Bow and the Milk rivers, drain southern Alberta to join the Missouri-Mississippi system that finally reaches the Caribbean Sea.

Most of the population of the two huge provinces is near the United States border, and up into central Alberta. Splendid highways, free of signboards and almost litter-free, connect the provinces. Three main routes slice through the Rocky Mountains: the Trans-Canada Highway, which crosses the Selkirks via Rogers Pass before topping the Continental Divide through Kicking Horse Pass out of Golden; the Southern Trans-Provincial Highway via Crowsnest Pass; and the Yellowhead Route, only officially

opened in 1970, the lowest pass at 3,711 feet. Along the highways, visitors' bureaus supply maps, brochures, and information.

Before you visit Western Canada, write for a free copy of the British Columbia Tourist Directory (Department of Travel Industry, Victoria) and the Alberta Tourist Guide (Alberta Government Travel Bureau, Edmonton). Information is also available at offices of the Canadian Government Travel Bureau, located in major U.S. cities.

Each directory lists accommodations with rates, provincial parks and other campgrounds, hours at ports of entry, customs requirements, fishing and hunting regulations, and such information as closing days for stores, locations of information centers, and golf courses. The British Columbia Directory also lists names of licensed guides (non-residents must be accompanied by guides when hunting big game in either province).

Entering Canada

You do not need a passport to enter Canada, but it is advisable to carry some identification, such as a birth certificate or a voter's registration card. A driver's license from any state allows you to drive in Canada. Although not required, it is wise to obtain from your

RENOVATED CITY HALL overlooks Victoria's Centennial Square, with its flowers and fountain.

MOUNT ROBSON, highest point in the Canadian Rockies at 12,972 feet, towers over this campsite.

insurance company a Canadian non-resident liability insurance card in case of accident. Boats entering Canadian waters must get a permit from customs.

Sports equipment (including camping gear, small boats, and cameras) is admitted without special papers, but must be declared upon entry and reported out when leaving the country. A visitor bringing in firearms or fishing tackle does not need a permit, but he must provide Canadian customs with a description of the equipment and serial numbers of the guns. Revolvers, pistols, and fully automatic firearms are prohibited.

Fishing and hunting fees

Fishing and hunting are governed by provincial laws, and licenses are required.

A non-Canadian fishing license costs $10 in British Columbia, or $3.50 for three days; $5 additional for steelhead fishing; no fee for fishing in tidal waters. A hunting license costs $25, plus $2 for migratory birds, and tag licenses for hunting various types of big game (ranging from 50 cents for black bear to $10 for grizzlies). All non-resident sportsmen are required to pay a trophy fee on any big-game animal killed (ranging from $5 for black bear to $75 for mountain sheep).

Alberta's alien fishing license costs $10, or $3 for three days. A hunting license costs $50, plus $2 for migratory birds, $2 for a wildlife certificate, and no trophy fee. A special $2 license is required to fish in Canadian national parks.

Customs

United States visitors may bring back merchandise up to a retail value of $100 free of duty after a stay of 48 hours (every 31 days), or to $10 if less than 48 hours.

Other useful information

British Columbia has a 5 per cent sales tax; Alberta has none.

When you cross from British Columbia into Alberta you move from Pacific Standard Time to Mountain Time, one hour later. From late April to late October British Columbia is on Daylight Saving Time.

Liquor by the bottle is sold in liquor stores (except on Sundays, when no liquor is sold). In a "licensed lounge" you may order beer, wine, and liquor by the glass; in a "licensed dining lounge" you order drinks with dinner.

BRITISH COLUMBIA

It was not until 1774 that the far northwest coast of North America was sighted by a European—the Spanish explorer Juan Perez. Four years later, as the American Colonies' War of Independence drew to a close in the east, Captain James Cook of the British Royal Navy planted his country's flag on the Western edge of Vancouver Island. With him as midshipman was George Vancouver, who was to return in 1792 to chart the adjacent coasts in detail.

One year later Alexander Mackenzie made the monumental first crossing of the northern Rockies and Coast Range to reach an arm of the sea near Bella Coola.

Other overland explorers followed to open up the vast western territory: David Thompson along the Columbia in 1806, Simon Fraser down the Fraser in 1808. Fur-trading posts and routes were quickly established.

From 1821 until 1849, the Hudson's Bay Company ruled this region. In 1846, the 49th parallel, accepted in the east as the Canadian border, was officially extended as such to the Pacific. Three years later, Vancouver Island became a crown colony.

In 1858, year of the Fraser-Cariboo gold rush, the mainland province of British Columbia (named by Queen Victoria) was established, with New Westminster as capital.

When the island colony merged with it eight years later, the capital moved to Victoria. Shortly after, on the condition that a national railway reach the coast,

British Columbia joined that new confederation, the Dominion of Canada.

British Columbia is a vast country; it could engulf Washington, Oregon, and California with plenty of room to spare.

This is a rugged, forested land, carpeted in spruce, fir, hemlock, and cedar, and drained by great rivers. Except for the rolling grasslands of the interior plateaus, mountains rib the province, holding long finger lakes in their valleys. Avid fishermen flock to roadside or fly-in lakes in search of fighting salmon, steelhead, Kamloops trout, or any of a dozen other varieties. Wildlife is abundant, and hunters comb the northern regions in search of trophy moose, elk, caribou, and other big game.

Offshore, numerous islands line the coast, providing a protected "inside passage" for ships bound for Alaska. The Strait of Georgia, with its sheltered harbors and forested islands, is a favorite of sailors.

More than 70 per cent of the province's approximately 2,000,000 people cluster in the southwest corner in and around Vancouver and Victoria, with enough left over to populate a handful of sizable coastal communities and the many small cities and towns that dot the interior valleys and northern plateaus.

The climate of the populated southern half generally mirrors that of the states immediately south. Summer is quite dry, and interior towns may be hot. September and October bring rain to coastal communities and the nip of frost inland.

From fall through spring the weather is usually wet and cool on the coast, with occasional short-lived snowfalls. Inland it will be cold, with frequent snow flurries. Interior lakes freeze over in winter; many stay frozen until May. Spring brings more rain to coastal communities.

WHISTLER MOUNTAIN'S broad snow fields offer great bowls of powder, vast expanses above timberline.

SOUTHWESTERN CORNER

Victoria's old-world charm and vigorous Vancouver highlight this area of magnificent scenery

The southwestern corner is the most populated area of British Columbia, yet it also contains some of the most beautiful primitive country in the province.

This water world, criss-crossed by a network of ferries and dotted with islands, is a favorite of fishermen and yachtsmen. The western shore of Vancouver Island with its isolated villages takes the brunt of the Pacific's wrath; the protected harbors on the eastern shore of the island and on the mainland enjoy a moderate year-round climate.

Magnificent mountain scenery is also found here, and this area is a favorite of mountaineers and skiers.

VICTORIA

Victoria, capital of British Columbia, Canada's third largest province, is at the southeastern tip of Vancouver Island, far into the southwestern corner of the vast province. Only 15 minutes by jet plane from Seattle, Victoria maintains an old world air that has long enchanted visitors; however, high rise buildings now crowd walls of ivy-covered stone.

Victorians take a tolerant attitude toward tourists who speak of their city as a little bit of England; this city of 130,000 people, British Columbia's capital since 1868, comes as near fitting the description as a traveler will find this side of the Old Country.

While horse-drawn tallyho and London bus, Tudor house and thatched roof replica may exist primarily for the visitor, afternoon high tea, luxuriant gardens, and a pace noticeably slower than that of mainland Vancouver across the Strait do not.

How to get there

You can reach Victoria only by air or sea.

Air Canada makes four daily flights from Seattle to the Victoria Airport 16 miles up-island, and 10 daily flights from Vancouver.

British Columbia Ferries operate daily year round service with frequent sailings from 6:15 A.M. to 10 P.M. (11 P.M. in summer) on the following routes:

From Tsawwassen (24 miles south of Vancouver) to Swartz Bay (20 miles north of Victoria). Crossing time: 1 hour 40 minutes.

From Horseshoe Bay (13 miles north of Vancouver) to Nanaimo (67 miles north of Vancouver). Crossing time: 1 hour 50 minutes.

Schedules are available from British Columbia Ferries, P.O. Box 1388, Victoria, British Columbia.

Canadian Pacific Steamships provide three daily trips (crossing time: 2 hours, 45 minutes) between Vancouver pier and Nanaimo; from May to late September you can make a special roundtrip day excursion from Seattle to Victoria on the *Princess Marguerite* (4 hours each way, 5 hours in Victoria), for $8 per person. (Regular one-way fare is $6, $8 for a car.) During the 5-hour interval, the ship makes one roundtrip between Victoria and Port Angeles, Washington.

Black Ball Transport travels between Victoria and Port Angeles, Washington, twice daily in winter, 4 times a day in summer (crossing time: 1 hour, 25 minutes).

INNER HARBOUR is the heart of Victoria. Ferries from Seattle and Port Angeles dock here, and water tours start from here. A new waterfront complex is now in the planning stage.

Washington State Ferries has daily year-round service, three trips daily in summer, from Anacortes, Washington (78 miles north of Seattle) to Sidney, B.C. (15 miles north of Victoria). Crossing time: 2½ to 3 hours.

One-way fares on the various ferries range from $2 to $2.95 per person, $5 to $6 per automobile. All schedules are available from the Victoria Visitors Bureau, 786 Government Street, Victoria.

The Inner Harbour

When you arrive on the *Princess Marguerite* or Black Ball's *M V Coho*, you land inside Victoria's charming little Inner Harbour. To the south stand the imposing Parliament Buildings, ahead, the rambling, ivy-covered Empress Hotel.

"Welcome to Victoria" is spelled out in flowers on the harbor's southern bank, an appropriate introduction to a city that every June hangs 650 gay baskets of brightly blooming flowers from its lampposts.

From fish'n'chips to Yorkshire pudding

Victoria has excellent hotel-motel accommodations (see the British Columbia Tourist Directory), and many eating places from fish-and-chip shops to elegant restaurants that feature seafood fresh from the ocean, or traditional English roastbeef and Yorkshire pudding, with perhaps an English trifle as a "sweet."

Although night life is not Victoria's main attraction, the downtown area has a supper club or two, and dancing in several hotel dining rooms. The Smile Show, patterned after a British Music Hall performance, is staged six nights a week at the Langham Court Theatre, a summer feature for nearly two decades.

Getting around Victoria

The Inner Harbour is the heart of the city, and tours start from here by Gray Line, Vancouver Island, and other coach lines, double-decker buses, and canopy-topped tallyhos. They all take a similar route through the parks, along blue bays, through lovely residential areas, and up the Saanich Peninsula.

If you want to go in your own car, ask the Victoria Visitors Bureau (across from the Empress Hotel) for a city map. Or hire a college student guide at the nearby red, white, and blue booth to accompany you on a walking or driving tour.

Exploring on foot

Victoria is a walking city, and many of the places you may want to visit are within a few blocks of the esplanade above the harbor.

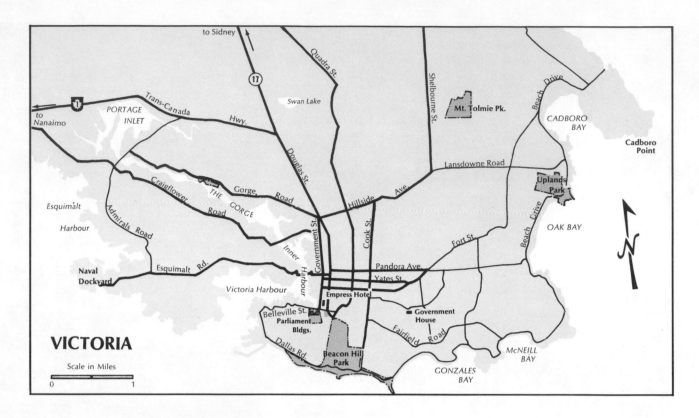

VICTORIA

Scale in Miles

0   1

HORSE-DRAWN TALLYHO tours start every 10 minutes from corner opposite Parliament Buildings.

The grand old Parliament Buildings, completed in 1897, are open to visitors Monday through Friday, and 20-minute tours start at 9:30 A.M. Visitors see the legislative chambers on the second floor in their 19th century setting of Italian marble and red velvet, where the Provincial Legislature meets from the last week of January to the week before Easter. Spectators may watch sessions from the galleries.

Heritage Court, in contrast to the massive, dark solidity of the Parliament Buildings, and just across the street from them, is architecturally airy and contemporary. A centennial project of 1968, the court contains the Provincial Museum, the Archives Building housing the Pacific North West Historical Library, and the Curatorial Building for research. At the court entrance rises the high, white carillon donated to the city by members of Victoria's Netherlands community.

Inside the elegant and spacious museum, the first floor's dominant exhibit is a great dugout with eight carved wooden figures of early Nootka whalers. Escalators take visitors to two more floors to see exhibits illustrating both the natural and cultural history of British Columbia. Realistic dioramas show wildlife of the province in natural habitat.

Free, the museum is open from 10 A.M. to 8:30 P.M. Monday through Saturday from June through September; 10 A.M. to 4:30 P.M. (closed Mondays) from October through May, and Sunday all year from 1 to 4:30 P.M.

The Archives Building has equally fascinating displays, among them maps, charts, pictures, ships' logs, and old journals of the Hudson's Bay Company.

Thunderbird Park, adjoining the court on Douglas Street, has a splendid collection of totem poles grouped to show styles of six major west coast Indian tribes: Haida, Kwakiutl, Tsimshian, Bella Coola, Nootka, and Coast Salish.

Helmcken House, built in 1852 and a museum of that era, is just around the corner at 638 Elliott Street, open 10 A.M. to noon, and 1:10 to 5 P.M. Tuesday through Sunday.

The Royal London Wax Museum, Douglas and Belleville Streets, has some 100 Josephine Tussaud figures from London, among them Abraham Lincoln, John Kennedy, Queen Victoria, King Henry VIII and his six wives, Napoleon, and the present Royal Family of Great Britain. Open daily from 9 A.M. to 10 P.M.

The Undersea Gardens in the Inner Harbour (open 10 A.M. to 9 P.M. daily) are 10 feet below the surface of the sea. Every hour a scuba diver brings unusual marine creatures—a wolf-eel and an octopus—for closeup views through the windows.

The Empress Hotel, Canadian Pacific Railway's "Dowager Empress," built in 1908 and given a recent $4 million renovation, dominates this area. Tea is served in the lobby between 3 and 5 P.M., an occasion with British overtones—a pot of tea, thin-sliced sandwiches, and small cakes.

Beacon Hill Park, edging the waters of the Strait of Juan de Fuca, has 154 acres of tree-shaded walks, and great masses of flowers. Swans from Queen Elizabeth's swannery in England glide on tiny, quiet lakes. A short stroll south from the Inner Harbour, the park borders Douglas Street.

Sightseeing by car

Five tours from 7 to 38 miles long are outlined on the back of the city map supplied at the Visitors Bureau. Yellow dots in the streets also indicate these routes. Signs topped with white seagulls indicate historical points of interest. Don't miss these stops:

Sealand, 1327 Beach Drive, adjoining the Oak Bay Marina and restaurant, has another exciting oceanarium, with dolphins, sea lions, cormorants, and other sea birds, and a performing killer whale (open 10 A.M. to 9 P.M. daily in July and August; in other months hours are 10 A.M. to 5 P.M. weekdays and Saturday, 1 to 5 P.M. Sunday).

The Uplands is Victoria's most elegant residential

THUNDERBIRD PARK, on Douglas Street, has a display of totems of six West Coast Indian tribes.

area. Drive its winding streets under the shade of great Garry oaks.

Government House, 1401 Rockland Avenue, residence of the Lieutenant-Governor of the province, opens its broad lawns and formal gardens to the public daily from dawn to dusk.

Craigdarroch Castle, 1050 Joan Crescent, a mammoth, red-roofed and turreted castle built by Robert Dunsmuir in 1851 for his homesick Scottish bride; open 9:30 A.M. to 4 P.M. Monday through Friday.

The Art Gallery of Greater Victoria, 1040 Moss Street, has fine permanent and traveling exhibits (open 11 A.M. to 5 P.M. Tuesday through Saturday, 2 to 5 P.M. Sunday). Free.

Olde England Inn, 429 Lampson Street, has an English village street of half-timbered houses, a replica of William Shakespeare's Stratford-on-Avon birthplace, and one of Anne Hathaway's thatched cottages. Cottage tours daily 8 A.M. to 10 P.M.

Point Ellice House, 2616 Pleasant Street, a century-old residence still occupied, has collection of Victorian furnishings (open daily 9 A.M. to 5 P.M.)

The University of Victoria occupies a green and spacious campus in the Gordon Head area. A delightful summer festival, Victoria Fair, is offered at the Phoenix Theatre on campus, where plays are presented in rotating repertory along with a series of musical recitals.

Shopping

Shopping is one of the rare treats for Victoria visitors. Conveniently concentrated along Government Street, starting at the Empress Hotel corner, are the shops to which American travelers flock. They carry a wonderful variety of china—Wedgwood, Spode, Royal Doulton, Royal Worcester, Minton, Irish Beleek, Royal Crown Derby, Staffordshire—and many patterns. China may be 20 to 40 per cent less expensive here because of duty paid in the United States.

Smart clothiers for men and women have English woolens and leathers, sweaters, kilts, and tartans from Scotland. One shop will supply your clan plaid if you are of Scottish descent. Another specializes in handwoven woolens in coat and suit lengths, another in linens from Ireland.

Cowichan sweaters, hand spun and hand knitted by Cowichan Indians of the Island, are made of gray,

WINDOW SHOPPING is a delight for Victoria visitors who look for antiques, crafts, and British imports.

OAK BAY MARINA harbors yachts, rental boats, a killer whale, and has an outstanding restaurant.

black, and white untreated wool. You will also find Haida totem poles and Eskimo soapstone carvings.

The big department stores (open 9 A.M. to 5:30 P.M., Thursday and Friday until 9 P.M.) are on Douglas Street, many antique centers and book shops on Fort Street, particularly between Vancouver and Cook Streets. Only a few small shops still observe the former Wednesday afternoon closing.

Two handsome squares

Centennial Square, the civic center, and Bastion Square, on the waterfront, have both emerged in recent years from formerly run-down areas.

Centennial Square, Government and Pandora Streets, includes the City Hall, built in 1878, and the McPherson Playhouse, a Pantages theater of 1912, both spruced up outside and refurbished inside. The playhouse is the theater for Vancouver Island's professional, regional theater.

Bastion Square at the foot of View Street, once a muddy hangout for gold prospectors and British remittance men, includes Village Fair, a charming old building housing boutiques and a restaurant.

The Maritime Museum, in the former courthouse in Bastion Square, has two floors of seafaring history, ship models, and salty exhibits that bring to life dramatic days of the naval and merchant fleets that sailed the British Columbia coast (open daily 10 A.M. to 5 P.M., and to 9 P.M. during July and August). Free.

Up the Saanich Peninsula

A pleasant, lazy loop trip up the Saanich Peninsula on Highway 17 to Wain Road, and back on West Saanich Road, passes famed Butchart Gardens. Or you might take the ferry at Brentwood Bay to Mill Bay, and return to Victoria via lovely Malahat Drive.

The Dominion Astrophysical Observatory, 10 miles north of Victoria on West Saanich Road, is open Monday through Friday, 9:30 A.M. to 4:30 P.M. From April through November the observatory is open Saturday evenings. You may look through the 72-inch telescope during demonstrations.

Boat tours and fishing

Ten cruises a day leave from the foot of the esplanade to tour harbor and gorge; others include Esquimalt Harbour.

BUTCHART GARDENS

The renowned Butchart Gardens, once a limestone quarry, now a tapestry of color spread across 25 acres of green hill and valley, are 13 miles north of Victoria off West Saanich Road.

The landscaping represents many regions: An English rose garden where every variety among some 2,000 bushes is marked; precise topiary and sculptured fountains in formal Italian design; lacquered bridges above a splashing stream in the Japanese garden.

A tearoom in the large residence, Benvenuto, serves lunch or tea between 11 A.M. and 5 P.M., and buffet supper from 5:30 to 7:30 P.M. during July and August.

Entertainment is offered on the stage of the band shell—music, revues, puppet shows—on summer evenings and Sunday afternoons, and lights go on throughout the gardens at dusk.

The gardens open daily at 9 A.M. from April through October. Closing times vary by month—in midsummer the gardens are open until 11 P.M., spring and fall closings are as early as 5 P.M.

Admission includes the shows from July 1 to Labor Day (adults $2, 13 to 17-year-olds $1.75, 5 to 12-year-olds 75 cents). Prices are lower in spring and autumn. In winter the gardens are open without charge from 9 A.M. to 4:30 P.M.

BUTCHART GARDENS' acres of green lawns and brightly blooming flowers cover old quarry.

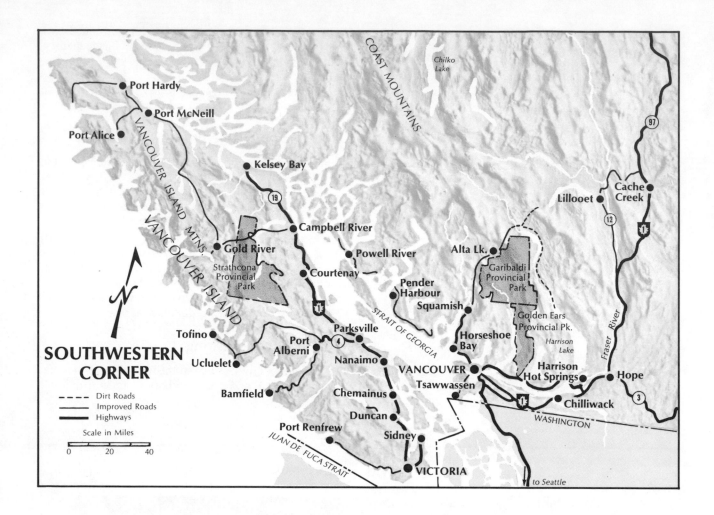

Boats with outboard motors, cabin cruisers, and guides may all be hired at various marinas for trolling great salmon waters. The cruiser *MV Lakewood* takes fishing parties out from Oak Bay Marina for 3 to 4-hour trips ($1.35 an hour).

Sports

None of Greater Victoria's nine elegantly maintained golf courses is municipally owned, but each is open to American visitors.

Sports with a foreign flavor include lacrosse at the Victoria Memorial Arena, and frequent cricket matches Saturday or Sunday afternoons in Beacon Hill or Windsor Parks. Behind the Crystal Gardens on Belleville Street, white-costumed lawn bowlers are often in action on weekends.

The Swiftsure Race

Memorial Day weekend brings Victoria's most colorful event, the Swiftsure Race. Sleek sailboats enter the harbor on Friday. Evening brings sunset ceremonies by the Royal Canadian Navy, and sea chanties sung by a male chorus, the Meistersingers.

Starting guns sound at 9 o'clock Saturday morning for the 136-mile race on Juan de Fuca Strait to Swiftsure Bank, 13 miles off the tip of Cape Flattery, where the lightship *Swiftsure* is anchored. By late Sunday, the yachts come sailing home.

VANCOUVER ISLAND

Vancouver Island, home to approximately 350,000 people, stretches northwest for 282 miles, paralleling British Columbia's mainland, bulging to 80 miles at its widest. Mountains sweep the length of the island hiding long, narrow lakes, and fiords deeply indent the rugged western coast. The mountains catch rain and westerly winds, causing the gentler southeast coast and its cluster of gulf islands to have balmy days long on sunshine.

For 215 leisurely miles, paved highway skirts the eastern shore from Victoria to Kelsey Bay, takeoff point by ferry for Prince Rupert and Alaska. First by Trans-Canada Highway 1 for 69 miles to Nanaimo, then by Provincial Highway 19 the rest of the way, it goes through woods where maple trees brighten the deeper green of fir and cedar, through pleasant towns beside the blue Strait of Georgia, and past crescent beaches where low tides uncover beds of oysters and clams. For anglers, the road leads always toward unparalleled fishing.

Side roads branch off to lakes, parks, campgrounds, and occasionally cut across the island from its mild-mannered side to the rain-slashed edge of the sea. All the way up-Island, the mainland mountains across the water reflect in soft azure haze the deep sapphire of the broad, island-dotted strait. Spring is a delightful time on Vancouver Island, when daffodils and lilacs bloom beside every farmhouse. Summer brings days in the 70's and 80's, and during autumn's quiet Indian summer, gold splashes the forest.

Along the way

Campers will find a dozen provincial campgrounds, starting with shady Goldstream Park 12 miles north-west of Victoria, and Bamberton Park, with its fine swimming beach, at Mill Bay. Accommodations range from unpretentious motels and fishing cabins to rambling, garden-framed lodges above the strait that have an old-world flavor.

Cowichan Bay is noted for its salmon fishing. To see its marina with row on row of fishing boats, turn off at Mill Bay onto Cowichan Bay Road. On the way back to the main highway at Duncan, about 10 miles from the Mill Bay turnoff, watch for the old stone church high above the road, built in 1870 by a Roman Catholic priest, the island's first church.

The Cowichan Forest Museum, one mile north of Duncan, displays the gear of early day logging—huge circular saws, donkey engines—and offers a mile-long ride behind a puffing steam locomotive (open May to September from 10 A.M. to 5:30 P.M.).

Nanaimo

Vancouver Island's second largest city, with a population of around 15,000, Nanaimo began in the mid-19th century with coal mining. Logs from surrounding forests now are responsible for its new rising waterfront skyline.

Earlier days are recalled in Piper Park with a steam locomotive once engaged in hauling coal, and in the attractive museum there, which houses the information center. Downtown, the old bastion, built in 1853 by the Hudson's Bay Company, still stands. Exhibits on three levels—the last by ship's ladder—illustrate those days. Open 10 A.M. to noon, 1 to 5 P.M., and 6:30 to 8:30 P.M. daily. There's no charge, but contributions are accepted.

North of Nanaimo, Parksville and Qualicum Beach are noted for their warm water beaches, and west from Parksville is one of the island's loveliest drives.

EARLY CHAPEL near Duncan was called Butter Church. Indian workers were paid in butter.

To the Albernis

For 29 miles, Highway 4 cuts through forests of fir to the Albernis, a pair of lively communities at the head of Alberni Inlet. Alberni supplies accommodations, and Port Alberni is its industrial twin, with its enormous McMillan and Bloedel mill complex.

On the way are 100 campsites and a lovely waterfall at Englishman River Park, 5 miles south of the highway on Errington Road. Little Qualicum Falls Park, 12 miles west of Parksville, has wide trails through an undergrowth of salal and fern below fir, cedar, and red-barked arbutus.

Cameron Lake, at 16 miles, cold and still, mirrors the wilderness about it, and just beyond is McMillan Park, with appropriately named Cathedral Grove, where centuries-old Douglas fir trees, reminiscent of California's redwoods, stand silent and tranquil.

Down to the sea by back road

Two roads go roller coasting over forested ridges to the western shore, one restricted to weekend use, rough going through backwoods country to Bamfield,

BUTTLE LAKE, 30-mile-long waterway in Strathcona Provincial Park, yields cutthroat and rainbow trout and Dolly Varden. Motorboats are allowed here, but they aren't bothersome.

a fishing village by the ocean. The other, partly paved but mostly gravel, passes Sproat and Kennedy Lakes, and reaches the coast in 67 miles. From here it is 5 miles south to the Indian fishing community, Ucluelet, and 21 miles north to Tofino along one of the province's finest beaches—clean-swept, wide, wave-rippled sand, where the surfing is special. Besides limited but good resort accommodations, Wickaninnish Beach Park has campsites and picnic tables.

Down to the sea by ship

The *MV Lady Rose,* a 100-foot-long mail, cargo, and passenger ship, makes twice-a-week roundtrips to Bamfield (and Sunday afternoons as well during July and August), and year-round Monday and Friday cruises to Ucluelet. From May 15 to September 30, she makes an extra trip on Wednesdays.

The sturdy diesel-powered vessel, built in Scotland, can carry 100 passengers and has a small snack bar. She sails from the foot of Argyle Street, Port Alberni, at 8 A.M., returning to port about 6 P.M. Indian families, loggers, and tourists make up the passenger list, and there's a friendly crew. An occasional loggers' camp is the only habitation along the narrow fiord.

Reserve ahead in midsummer by writing to Alberni Marine Transportation, Ltd., Box 188, Port Alberni, British Columbia, or by telephoning 723-5788.

On up-Island

Courtenay and Comox, famed for their offshore trolling waters, cater to fishermen with beach-side cottages, launching ramps, and marinas. In December, fine family skiing starts on Mount Becher, 12 miles west of Courtenay.

Miracle Beach Park, 14 miles north of Courtenay, is one of the island's best campgrounds. Its Nature House, open daily during summer, shows types of trees, ferns, seaweed, birds, and marine life of the locale.

Campbell River

Salmon fishing is superb up and down the Strait of Georgia, but Campbell River calls itself the "world salmon fishing capital," and during the height of the fishing season, the community's population of some 8,000 virtually triples. Excellent accommodations are provided, from modern mid-town motor hotels to roomy lodges above Discovery Passage.

Boats, tackle, and guides are available at marinas and resorts. For example, 16-foot outboards, including gear, bait, gas, oil, and guide, rent for $6.50 to $7 an hour; 34-foot cabin cruisers including all facilities, for $140 a day.

Arrangements may also be made for trips to many

TRAWLERS docked at Campbell River harbor are a familiar sight.

BLUE WATERS of the Strait of Georgia are ideal for sailing among the forested Gulf Islands, just east of Vancouver Island.

parts of the province by float plane. Write Guides Unlimited, 1084 Island Highway, Campbell River, British Columbia, for information.

Highway 19 continues for 50 miles from Campbell River to Kelsey Bay, lumber mill town where the *Queen of Prince Rupert* leaves for her trip up the Inside Passage.

Strathcona Provincial Park

A road, paved most of the way, coils westward for 57 miles to Gold River, slicing through the northern part of wild and lovely 561,179-acre Strathcona Provincial Park. Upper and Lower Campbell Lakes lie just northeast of it.

Strathcona Park Lodge on Buttle Lake, about half way between Campbell River and Gold River, offers rooms, cottages, dining room, campground, boat rentals, and guides.

From Gold River, a limited access logging road, eventually to be a public highway, winds north to isolated Beaver Cove, Port McNeill, Port Hardy, and Port Alice at the edge of the Pacific.

The Gulf Islands

Clustered off the southeastern coast of Vancouver Island, some 100 islands mushroom out of the Strait of Georgia only a few miles northwest of the San

SEA VOYAGE INTO HISTORY

Twice a week from June 28 to September 13, the *Uchuck III*, a stout, sea-going freighter, carries tourists to Nootka Sound, birthplace of British Columbia. Originally a mine sweeper, she now takes cargo and passengers to isolated settlements at the head of narrow arms of the sea.

On her tourist cruises, she leaves every Wednesday and Saturday at 1:15 P.M. from the head of Muchalat Inlet, 8 miles west of Gold River, stops for one hour at Friendly Cove before continuing on the 25-mile run to Nootka Sound, and arrives back at the docks at 6:15 P.M.

Captain James Cook of the British Royal Navy landed in Friendly Cove in 1778, the first white man to set foot on Vancouver Island. Here he traded with the Indians for sea otter furs, which later were to bring a far-flung trade to this wilderness coast. Here he repaired his leaking ship, *HMS Resolution,* and late in April of '78 sailed into Arctic waters in search of the Northwest Passage.

A trip on the twisting fiord is an adventure in itself. Passengers line the railings to watch the loading and unloading in port.

You don't need a car to make the trip. Vancouver Island Coach Lines leaves Campbell River at 9 A.M. for Gold River, allowing time for lunch at the attractive inn there before boarding ship.

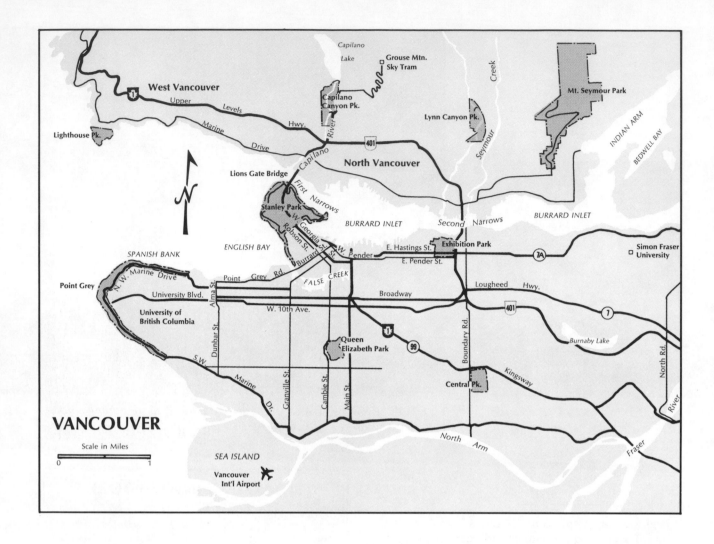

VANCOUVER

Scale in Miles
0 — 1

Juan group in Washington. Some of the Gulf Islands are tiny, tree-tufted mounds, others large like Saltspring Island, where wooded slopes rise some 2,400 feet. Protected by the mountains of Vancouver Island, and with only 20 to 25 inches of rainfall a year, the Gulf Islands are the delight of yachtsmen, who nose their craft into endless quiet coves.

Approximately 3,000 people live on Saltspring Island, which has a score of resorts, from housekeeping cottages to American plan inns, a 9-hole golf course, and a provincial campground on Mount Maxwell, with 15 campsites, half a dozen picnic tables, and a terrific view. Galiano Island also has a golf course and resorts. Some islands are privately owned, but most are uninhabited.

Boating

Hundreds of American boatsmen cross the international boundary every year to explore these waters and to fish. Pleasure craft must register at a Canadian Customs office at Bedwell Harbour on South Pender

Island (open May through September), or Sidney on Vancouver Island. On their return, American boats must check out with Canadian Customs, and check in again at the nearest American office, usually Friday Harbor or Roche Harbor on San Juan Island.

Island hopping by ferry

You don't need a boat, however, to visit the islands. British Columbia Ferries connect Saturna, Mayne, Galiano, North Pender, and Saltspring Islands with the Tsawwassen terminal on the mainland, and with Swartz Bay, north of Victoria. Others operate between Crofton on Vancouver Island and Saltspring Island, Chemainus and Thetis Island, and Nanaimo and Gabriola Island.

A half-day cruise, with stops at four islands, leaves Swartz Bay at 9:20 A.M., returns at 1:35 P.M.; takes off again at 2:30, and returns at 6:55 P.M. (Fares are $2 for the roundtrip.) For schedules, write to British Columbia Ferries, 816 Wharf Street, Victoria, British Columbia.

VANCOUVER

Vancouver, Canada's third largest city, is one of the great seaports of the world, and water and mountains give it one of the world's most dramatic settings. The Strait of Georgia reaches a long arm round it on the north, the Fraser River bounds it on the south, and mountains to north and east tower above it.

This was what Captain George Vancouver saw when, in 1792 in *HMS Discovery*, carrying 100 men and 20 guns, he discovered and sailed up the inlet around which the city is built.

Now, with a fast changing 20th century skyline, tall apartment buildings ring the shore of Vancouver's outer harbor, and tubular structures of concrete, steel, and glass climb the downtown hills. Frequent parks, both large and small, break the pattern of city streets with patches of green, and roses bloom from April into autumn. And there's an annual contest for the first daffodils grown in open gardens, with judging on March 1.

A young city, incorporated in 1886, Vancouver now covers 44 square miles, and has a population of nearly 500,000. Greater Vancouver, with almost twice as many people as in the city itself, includes North and West Vancouver, Burnaby, Richmond, New Westminster, Coquitlam, Port Moody, and Delta.

Ever since the Canadian Pacific Railway's first trans-Pacific ship *Abyssinia* docked at the line's new pier in 1887 with a cargo of tea, 22 first class passengers, and eight Chinese in steerage, Vancouver trade has grown through its shipping. Now Vancouver is the world's greatest wheat port, with lumber its second most important commodity.

The massive port development of Roberts Bank at the mouth of the Fraser River, now well underway, will be used as a terminal for shipping coal to Japan.

LIONS GATE BRIDGE arches 200 feet in mid-span above First Narrows of Vancouver's Burrard Inlet.

In and out of Vancouver

Nine major airlines serve Vancouver. The spacious Vancouver International Airport terminal, built at a cost of more than $30 million, opened on Sea Island, 11 miles south of town, in October, 1968.

Both the Canadian Pacific and the Canadian National Railways operate daily service across the continent; Pacific Great Eastern has daily service to Fort St. John, and the Great Northern makes two trips a day between Seattle and Vancouver.

British Columbia Ferries schedule 14 crossings a day between Tsawwassen (20 miles south of the city) and Swartz Bay, departure point for Victoria on Vancouver Island, and a dozen trips a day each way between Vancouver and Nanaimo.

Two roundtrips a day to Nanaimo are operated by 35-passenger Hovercraft from the foot of Granville Street. The craft, which rides a cushion of air four feet above the water, makes the trip in 50 minutes.

Accommodations

Vancouver provides comfortable to luxurious accommodations. Many motels are located beside highways coming into the city, particularly along Kingsway, or Highway 99, but the big luxury hotels, like the old Vancouver, which remodeled its 315 rooms in recent years when Hilton took it over, are concentrated downtown. Although Vancouver offers 6,500 rooms to visitors, it is advisable to book ahead from June to August. During the spring, a wider choice of accommodations and off-season prices prevail.

Things to do

Probably no city presents visitors with more varied and easily accessible recreation. You can swim, fish, hike, golf, ride horseback, and even ski within actual minutes of the center of the city.

Daily cruises range from one-hour spins to all-day

STANLEY PARK

Stanley Park is special. Its accessibility, its waterside setting, its combination of forest and suburban facilities make it so. Vancouver residents make great use of it, tourists visit it, highways cut through and around it, yet it never seems crowded.

Almost an island, this 1,000-acre peninsula that bulges into Burrard Inlet is a 15-minute stroll from the center of town (though Vancouverites don't stroll; they walk with a zest that is a noticeable characteristic of Western Canadians).

Stanley Park Drive rims the park; 27 miles of trails weave through its woods of red cedar, Douglas fir, hemlock, poplar, and maple. Grassy slopes give ample space for picnic tables.

At Coal Harbour, you can rent a catamaran for $5 an hour; on Lost Lagoon, rowboats rent for $1 an hour.

Focal point in the immaculately maintained zoo is the aquarium. Here "Skana," a huge killer whale, amiably stages a spectacular performance at meal time (every 2 hours on week days, hourly on weekends) for bleacher spectators. There's no charge for the zoo, but the aquarium costs $1.50 for adults and 25 cents for children.

An 18-hole pitch and putt golf course, a 9-hole putting green, 27 tennis courts, horseshoe pitches, and shuffleboard are here for visitor use, also a grass hockey pitch, a rugby field, and two cricket pitches. Most Saturday afternoons you'll see a cricket match underway at Brockton Oval.

Special love of young visitors is the gaily canopied toy train that toots through the shady woods, passing pens of farm animals, a den of snowy Arctic wolves, and possibly a peacock beside the tracks spreading its brilliant tail. The train operates from dawn to dusk daily in summer, weekends only (weather permitting) during the rest of the year.

When the day is over at Stanley Park, an old muzzle-loading cannon sounds off at exactly 9 o'clock. It used to boom the fishermen home. Now, traditionally, Vancouverites set their watches by it.

STANLEY PARK has something for everyone: a lagoon, totem poles, rustic pathways, an aquarium and a zoo, beaches, picnic grounds, swimming pools, and a sports area.

STEEL AND GLASS skyscrapers rise higher and higher on Vancouver's skyline. View is looking northwest toward North Vancouver; Stanley Park juts out into Burrard Inlet from left.

trips. There is horse racing at Exhibition Park, cricket on Brockton Oval in Stanley Park, fine stores for shoppers, and a great choice of cuisine in restaurants ranging from dockside ships to roof-top dining rooms.

How to see it all

Several coach lines offer tours of city and suburbs, the Gray Line providing a wide choice of local excursions from 2½-hour drives to overnight package tours to Victoria.

British Columbia Hydro and Power Authority operates convenient bus service. To find out where and when to catch what bus, telephone 261-4211. Fare is 20 cents. On Sundays, a 50-cent pass lets you ride as long and on as many buses as you like. On retail shopping days, a 25-cent downtowner pass does the same from 9 A.M. to 3:30 P.M. downtown.

The usual car rentals are available at prices similar to those in the States. Taxi fare is 55 cents plus 40 cents per mile after the first mile, or $4 per hour, whichever is the greater.

Downtown on foot

Canadians, like their British forebears, are great walkers, and Vancouver is a walker's city. The down-town section is a peninsula 20 blocks long at its longest point, 17 blocks wide at its broadest part. Most of the city's best hotels, and many of its best restaurants are along or just off West Georgia Street, its big stores and its cinemas along Granville Street. Stanley Park is a 15-minute walk northwest from the center of this downtown area, Chinatown a 15-minute walk in the other direction. The following are all within this easy walking area.

The Greater Vancouver Visitors and Convention Bureau, 650 Burrard St., one-half block down from the Hotel Vancouver, should be your first stop. Here are free maps, brochures, and pleasantly proffered information. Summer hours: 9 A.M.-7 P.M., Monday through Saturday; noon-5 P.M., Sundays and holidays. In winter: 9 A.M.-5 P.M., Monday through Saturday. (Telephone, 682-2222.)

For information about travel elsewhere in the province, accommodations, fishing, and hunting, go next door to the British Columbia Information Centre, 652 Burrard St. (Neither office provides reservation service but will assist in finding accommodations.)

The B. C. Hydro-Authority Building at Burrard and Nelson Streets (the building that is always lighted at night) invites visitors to see the view from its 19th floor any time between 9 A.M. and 4:30 P.M., Monday through Friday. The view is free and terrific.

The P & O-Orient and Canadian Pacific Railway piers are always good for a closeup of harbor activities. From the ramp at the foot of Burrard Street you see logs being lifted from the water by giant claws to fill the holds of great black freighters, and hefty sacks of grain being loaded aboard ship. Crowds always gather to see the P & O liners nose into port, and on departure days, bands play as passengers board.

The Vancouver Art Gallery, 1145 West Georgia St., includes paintings by the late Emily Carr, much-admired British Columbia artist, in its permanent collection. Open 10 A.M. to 5 P.M. Monday through Saturday, and to 10 P.M. Wednesday and Friday; 2 to 5 P.M. Sunday.

The Gallery of British Columbia Arts, 1974 West Georgia St., at the entrance to Stanley Park, features paintings, pottery, and sculpture of local artists. Open 9:30 A.M. to 5 P.M. weekdays, 2 to 6 P.M. Sundays.

The Queen Elizabeth Theatre and Playhouse, 649 Cambie St., an elegant three-level complex, is a 5-minute walk from Hotel Vancouver. The smaller theater, which houses the Playhouse Theatre Company, adjoins the Queen Elizabeth's 2,800-seat auditorium, where Vancouver's Symphony Orchestra and Opera Association perform. The theater block includes a spacious, landscaped plaza, a restaurant, and lower-level parking.

Chinatown is the second largest on the North American continent (around 16,000 Chinese-Canadians live in the area). Some excellent Chinese restaurants, and tiny intriguing shops are on East Pender in the three blocks between Carrall Street and Gore Avenue.

Shop here for jade, silver, ivory, antique china, Oriental curios, and see the "smallest store in the world," a 4-foot-wide key-making shop on the southwest corner of East Pender and Carrall Streets.

Other shopping

Shopping is largely concentrated in the eastern half of the downtown peninsula, the large department stores like Hudson's Bay and Eatons, along Granville and Hastings Streets.

Department stores are open from 9 A.M. to 5:30 P.M., and some stay open until 9 P.M. on Fridays.

Specialty shops that feature British woolens, Irish linens, English china, Eskimo and British Columbia Indian crafts dot West Georgia Street and side streets.

Special Vancouver finds include carved wooden totem poles ranging in price from $1.95 to $1,000; totems of black argillite and decorative prints from the Haida Indians of the Queen Charlotte Islands; gray soapstone bird and animal carvings made by Eskimos of Quebec and the Northwest Territories, and red cedar masks made by the Squamish Indians of British Columbia. And if you want a bear rug, Vancouver is the place to look for it.

Be sure to stroll along Robson Street—Robsonstrasse they call it in Vancouver—between Hornby and Thurlow Streets. In tiny shops you'll find teakwood crafts from Norway, basketry from Mexico,

EXHIBITION PARK horse racing lasts from May to October; other sports—football, hockey, and lacrosse—are also played here.

CHINATOWN is fun for browsing. Goods range from food to jade.

brass from India, silks from Japan, great lengths of sausages in the windows of delicatessens that sell European cheeses; Turkish and Guatemalan coffee, Ceylon and Irish tea among dozens of varieties in that favorite tourist mecca, Murchie's Tea House. In small cafes you'll be served German schnitzel or Hungarian goulash, and in an Austrian konditorei you'll savor elaborate tortes and melting chocolate pastries.

Vancouver by car

Some lovely scenic drives swing through Vancouver, climb the foothills of the Coast Range across the harbor, and take in the pastoral country of the Fraser River delta.

Marine Drive, curling around Point Grey past the University of British Columbia, is one of the city's most scenic roads. Cross the Burrard Street Bridge and turn right on Cornwall, but before you go on, stop at the complex of planetarium, Centennial and Maritime Museums at the foot of Cypress Street.

The Centennial Museum, in an elegantly contemporary building, traces the history of the Indians of British Columbia and of the immigrants who followed. Summer hours are 10 A.M. to 10 P.M. daily.

The planetarium has a circular theater that seats 270 people. Shows are given four times daily (except Mondays from late June to September, less frequently the rest of the year). Fee includes admission to the museum.

The Maritime Museum, just beyond the Planetarium, has an excellent collection of ship models, and houses the RCMP schooner, *St. Roch*, famed for her two voyages, east to west and west to east, through the Arctic Northwest Passage (open 10 A.M. to 10 P.M. daily). You pass Kitsilano Beach, a popular one for swimming, and follow Point Grey Road.

Hastings Mill Store at the foot of Alma Street, was one of the few buildings left when fire all but destroyed the new settlement of Vancouver in 1886. A museum now, it is open from 10 A.M. to 4 P.M. daily, June 1 to September 15.

From Alma, turn right on 4th Avenue and go to Marine Drive. The drive passes Locarno and Spanish Banks beaches, and climbs above English Bay.

Nitobe Memorial Gardens, just off the highway (open 1 to 4 P.M. weekdays, 1 to 5 P.M. weekends) is a charming glimpse of Japan. Bridges arch above still ponds, stone lanterns mark meandering paths, and an authentic tea house is hidden in a leafy corner. (No admission charge weekdays, but 25 cents for adults, 10 cents for youngsters on weekends.)

Totem Park, a little farther on, represents a section of a Haida Indian village of the Queen Charlotte Islands. It has a long house (dwelling), a smaller grave house, and both family and funeral totem poles.

The University of British Columbia's 1,000-acre campus extends from Point Grey to gates on West 10th Avenue. See its impressive buildings, the sunken rose garden, the Olympic-size Empire Pool (open to the public), the 18-hole golf course and lovely residences of its Endowment Lands. Around 17,000 students attend the university.

The Museum of Anthropology in the basement of the University Library has a fine collection of Kwakiutl carvings (open daily except Wednesday and Sunday from 1 to 5 P.M., also Tuesday evenings from 7 to 9, free).

Follow Southwest Marine Drive around the point; take 41st Avenue, next turn left on Cambie to 33rd.

Queen Elizabeth Park on "Little Mountain," highest point in Vancouver, has formal gardens planted in former rock quarries, and a huge outdoor conservatory featuring plants of three climatic zones. Thirty-five acres here display trees and shrubs of the Northwest. Early June is a particularly lovely time when rhododendrons make a great splash of color.

North on Cambie and across Connaught Bridge leads back to town.

Exhibition Park

Most of Vancouver's chief sporting events, including a long season of horse racing, take place in Exhibition Park, comprised of 180 acres off East Hastings between Renfrew and Cassiar Streets.

Here are the Empire Stadium, home of the B.C.

NITOBE GARDENS offer the stroller quiet pathways, reflecting ponds, arched bridges, a tea house.

Lions, Vancouver's football team; and the Pacific Coliseum, where the Canucks (hockey) and the Curlings (lacrosse) play.

Every Vancouver visitor should see the giant topographical map of the province in the British Columbia Building here. You view it from a platform which moves slowly across the 80 by 76-foot map, made of nearly 100,000 pieces of plywood, as a guide explains its simulated mountain ranges and rivers, its islands and inlets (open 11 A.M. to 5 P.M., free).

The north shore

Nearly a quarter of a million people live on the north shore of Burrard Inlet, Vancouver's deep water harbor. The Capilano River divides North and West Vancouver, both of which have attractive residential areas, fine accommodations, and excellent restaurants.

The Upper Levels Highway slices across the foothills, and continues to Howe Sound. Side roads lead to hiking trails, ski slopes, and all-year fishing.

Horseshoe Bay, about 13 miles northwest of downtown Vancouver via the Upper Levels Highway, is popular for fishing, boating, dining, or just for the drive. Rental boats, tackle, and guides are available.

On salmon derby days, the Sound is speckled with boats. There's an annual British Columbia derby, with prizes totaling $50,000, and another August competition sponsored by the *Vancouver Sun* newspaper.

British Columbia Ferries operates daily service from Horseshoe Bay to Nanaimo, Vancouver Island; to Langdale on the mainland's Sunshine Coast, and 8 trips a day (9 on weekends) to forested Bowen Island, locale of summer homes and picnic grounds.

If you return via lower level Marine Drive, you can picnic and swim at Whytecliff Park, and visit Lighthouse Park, a quiet bit of unspoiled forest.

Capilano Canyon is a popular North Shore destination for its exciting suspension bridge. Capilano Park is about 1½ miles north of Lions Gate Bridge.

Cleveland Dam, on up Capilano Road, backs the Capilano River into a lake, main source of Vancouver's soft mountain water. Standing up sharp and clear behind it are the twin "couchant" lions, snow-topped peaks from which the harbor takes its name, the Lions Gate. Two miles further north is the lower terminus for the Grouse Mountain sky tram.

HORSESHOE BAY, north of Vancouver, is a favorite of fishermen. Here the ferry from Nanaimo is just sailing into the harbor.

CAPILANO bridge sways as you cross; river is 210 feet below.

Lynn Canyon Park, 2½ miles north of the Second Narrows Bridge, also has a suspension bridge, shorter (110 feet long), but also exciting, and free.

Mount Seymour, in Mount Seymour Provincial Park's 8,000 acres of forest, has trails, picnic spots, and a chair lift that operates all year to a chalet at the top. A paved mountain road twists for 8 miles through the park to a paved parking area where the lift begins.

Family skiing is the specialty at Mount Seymour, which operates daily in winter from 8:30 A.M. to 4 P.M., with skiing under lights from 7 to 10 o'clock on Tuesday, Wednesday, and Thursday nights (call 929-1040 for ski and road conditions).

Chair lift hours from December to April are 9 A.M. to 10 P.M. weekdays, 8:30 A.M. to 4 P.M. weekends. From April to December the lift operates daily from noon to sunset with weekend operations beginning at 10 A.M.

Garibaldi Park

Garibaldi Provincial Park, 70 miles north of Vancouver, is more and more a favorite mountain destination since it became Canada's bid for the 1976 Winter Olympics. Ski lifts glide up Whistler Mountain from a base elevation of 2,140 feet to 6,420 feet. The drop down—5 miles of skiing—is the longest vertical drop on the North American continent. Daily operation begins in December, and lasts until July on the upper slopes, when glacier skiing by helicopter is at its best.

Whistler lifts go up in two stages, first by 4-passenger gondola, then by double chair lift. These operate every summer weekend, too, from 9 A.M. to 3:30 P.M. Summer vacationers are finding the Alta and Green Lakes area at the base of Whistler as appealing as do skiers, and June ski class students ski in the morning, and swim, sail, fish, or ride horseback in the afternoon.

How to get there. The Pacific Great Eastern Railway leaves Vancouver daily at 8 A.M., arrives at Alta Lake station, near the base of Whistler Mountain, at 10:40 A.M., leaves Alta Lake for Vancouver at 6:53 P.M.

The 1½-hour summer season drive up Highway 99 to Alta Lake is one of the loveliest in the Vancouver area. Curving around rugged cliffs, the highway climbs high above Howe Sound, the mountains ahead forming a dramatic backdrop.

GROUSE MOUNTAIN

Vancouver's Grouse Mountain is a unique attraction—skiing 15 minutes from downtown, with all the city at your feet.

"Grouse," as most Vancouverites call it, is one of the coast mountains (4,103 feet) that rise abruptly above North Vancouver. To get there, drive across Lions Gate Bridge, turn up Capilano Road to the lower terminus of the Skytram at a 965-foot elevation (parking here for 900 cars). Grouse Mountain Resorts operates daily bus service from downtown hotels, and city buses also have daily service to Grouse. You can pick up a schedule at the Visitors Bureau.

The skyride operates all year from 9 A.M. to midnight every day of the year.

Now the excitement begins. You step into a 50-passenger, glass-enclosed aerial tramway that lifts you on a fast, 5-minute ride, sometimes nearly 200 feet above the ground, to the 3,590-foot terminus far above the city.

As you swing smoothly up—and sometimes it seems almost straight up—the view below stretches wider and wider until, from the cantilevered decks of the modern chalet at the top, you see all of Vancouver—its suburbs, its waterways, the flat delta of the Fraser River, the outline of Vancouver Island across the Strait of Georgia, and, on clear days, the Olympic Mountains and Mount Baker in Washington. At night, the twinkling lights of city and ships create an unforgettable scene.

Snowfall at the top of Grouse averages about 13 feet. Two chair lifts, T-Bar and ski tows operate on varied slopes. The "Inferno Run," a 60 per cent grade on the northeast side of the mountain into the Blueberry Bowl, is the catch-your-breath one.

The ski resort has ski and souvenir shops, cafeteria, Bavarian beer stube, and night club dining room. Skiing goes on from 9 A.M. to 10 P.M. seven days a week from December 1 to May 1.

GONDOLA RIDERS have a panorama of city, harbor, and Fraser River delta as the car ascends.

GARIBALDI PARK draws hikers in summer. Black Tusk juts against the skyline at left. You'll find wildflowers here in midsummer.

HARRISON HOT SPRINGS guests enjoy swimming or sunning.

Where to stay. Most of the dozen lodges near Whistler, and resorts on the lakes, offer year-around accommodations. Average cost of a cabin for 6 people is $20 a night. Many condominiums are also being built. Alice Lake Park, north of Squamish, has 94 campsites.

Other Garibaldi areas. The park has three other developed regions, one at Diamond Head, which has a Norwegian style chalet at a 5,000-foot elevation. (The last 7 miles into the chalet are by jeep or snowmobile provided by the resort.) Diamond Head has great cross-country skiing from December through May, and mountain climbing (including 8,787-foot-high Mount Garibaldi) from late July to October.

The Black Tusk region, accessible by trail or float plane, and Cheakamus Lake, reached by logging road and trail, are the other two developed areas. Alpine meadows carpeted with wildflowers in midsummer characterize them all.

The Sunshine Coast

The fiord-indented shore north of Vancouver known as the Sunshine Coast is for those who like salt water and mountain scenery mixed with quiet back roads, not too many people, and an overall emphasis on fishing. One hundred miles of coastline and two leisurely ferry crossings make a fine weekend introduction to the region. Or, by taking the ferry from Powell

River to Comox, Vancouver Island, you can make a loop trip around both shores of the lovely Strait of Georgia.

The first ferry crossing is from Horseshoe Bay to Langdale, popular recreation center. Ferries leave about every two hours from 7:55 A.M. until 9:45 P.M. for the 55-minute ride. The next is across Jervis Inlet from Earls Cove to Saltery Bay (50 minutes).

Highway 101 follows the coastline through small communities like Sechelt (500 population), and Pender Harbour, once a small fishing port now virtually taken over by tourists and anglers. At any of these coastal towns, it is easy to arrange a charter salmon fishing trip. Each town has its own marina.

Powell River is the paper mill town. The McMillan and Bloedel plant produces some 600,000 tons of newsprint a year; tours are available.

All the way, side roads lead to hidden coves and rocky beaches, where oyster beds are exposed at low tide. For more information about this region, write the Sunshine Coast Tourist Association, 6807 Wharf St., Powell River, British Columbia.

To Harrison and back

A good way to sample the Fraser River valley is to drive the south shore to Rosedale via the Trans-Canada Highway, cross the mile-long bridge above

PENDER HARBOUR, a quiet town on the mainland's Sunshine Coast, is a popular anchorage for yachtsmen. Fishermen can charter or rent boats in most coastal fishing towns.

the Fraser to Agassiz, visit Harrison Hot Springs, and return along the north shore through Mission City on the Lougheed Highway, about 150 miles in all.

At New Westminster, British Columbia's third largest city, and provincial capital from 1859 to 1868, see the beautiful gardens in Queens Park, and the Japanese Gardens next to the City Hall at Royal Avenue and 6th Street. Irving House, 302 Royal Ave., built in 1862, houses a museum portraying life a century ago. Summer hours are 11 A.M. to 5 P.M., Tuesday through Sunday; winter hours, 2 to 4 P.M. weekends.

Add an extra 10 miles to the trip to savor the serenity of the pastoral delta by taking the King George Highway south from New Westminster to New McLellan Road, and turn left. The road connects with Highway 1 again a few miles west of Abbotsford.

Two small Fraser tributaries, the Serpentine and the Nicomekl, narrow and slow-paced as English trout streams, wind through the valley. Both have good salmon runs in autumn.

Harrison Hot Springs, British Columbia's most famed spa, is a few miles north of Agassiz at the southern tip of Harrison Lake. Built in 1926, the resort added a $3 million extension in 1969. Mineral hot springs fill its two indoor pools and heat its outdoor pool. Trail rides, sailing, lake cruises, golf, and swimming are part of Harrison holidays.

Simon Fraser University

The 1,200-acre campus of Simon Fraser University high on Burnaby Mountain is a stimulating place to visit. (Go out East Hastings, south on Sperling Avenue, and right on Curtis Street.)

Opened in 1965, the university operates on a year-around schedule. Strikingly contemporary, its handsome buildings are of modular design that allow walking from one area to another always under shelter.

Special events

Something special is nearly always going on in the Vancouver area. Watch for these: New Westminster's 4-day May fete, based on traditional English May day festivals; the Caledonian Games in Burnaby, Abbotsford's International Air Show, both in August, and the Loggers' Sports Day in Squamish on the first Saturday in August. Vancouver's July Sea Festival includes a week of nautical events climaxed with a bathtub race across the Gulf of Georgia from Nanaimo.

Biggest event in the province is the Pacific National Exhibition at Exhibition Park during the last two weeks of August, annually attended by more than a million people. The year is traditionally brought to a close when the Christmas Carol Ship tours Vancouver's inner and outer harbors, as carolers aboard ship sing out the Yuletide message.

SOUTHEASTERN BRITISH COLUMBIA

Follow the mighty rivers into resort and Kamloops trout country

The southeastern portion of British Columbia is crossed by two major highways, Trans-Canada Highway 1, and the Southern Trans-Provincial Highway 3.

THE TRANS-CANADA HIGHWAY

Trans-Canada Highway 1 is the longest paved highway in the world, stretching for 4,787 miles from Victoria, British Columbia, to St. Johns, Newfoundland. As it cuts across southern British Columbia, it traverses the great variety of terrain that is characteristic of this vast province.

From the rich delta of the Fraser River, Highway 1 travels on high, wide curves through the rugged canyons of the Fraser and the Thompson Rivers, traverses the land of the big ranches, big lakes, big Kamloops trout, and swings on easy grades through three national parks before it meets the Jasper-Banff Highway at Lake Louise in Alberta.

Highway 1 is the base from which other important routes east of Vancouver diverge. Roads drop south like trailing ribbons to connect with Highway 3, the Southern Trans-Provincial route which winds close to the Canadian boundary, with 13 points of entry along the border of Washington, Idaho, and Montana.

Hope

The Fraser makes its sharp westward turn toward the sea at Hope, 96 miles east of Vancouver. Fort Hope was founded in 1848, but the Hudson's Bay factor actually called it Esperance, the French word for Hope. First it was a depot for fur brigades, later for gold miners. Christ Church, built in 1861 and now restored, is reminiscent of the gold era.

Yale

Fifteen miles north on the Fraser River, Yale was the end of navigation for the steamboats that used to carry prospectors upriver from Vancouver (providing the boats got that far without blowing up). Yale also has its own quaint church, Saint John the Divine, built by the Royal Engineers in 1860.

Hell's Gate

North from Yale, the original Cariboo Wagon Road hugged the ledges of the Fraser River Canyon. Now the broad, paved highway sweeps high above it. Three miles beyond Spuzzum, you look down from a high cliff into famous Hell's Gate. The Fraser, squeezed between narrowing walls of rock, wells up into a turmoil of swirling, silt-laden water; sometimes, during spring freshets, it swells to a depth of 170 feet.

When the river is low in late summer, you can see the concrete fishways built along either side of Hell's Gate to facilitate the return of spawning salmon to the place of their birth. A path drops down 600 feet from the highway to a platform above them. But it is a steep and somewhat risky hike.

AERIAL FERRY near Boston Bar can carry one car or 40 passengers.

NINE MILE CANYON BRIDGE is north of Boston Bar on Highway 1 along the Fraser River. It shortened Trans-Canada Highway 9 miles.

Aerial ferry

Check your road map, and be on the lookout for Boston Bar so you won't miss seeing the aerial cage that swings across the canyon to North Bend. The ferry takes one car at a time, transporting it airily for 900 feet on cables 1¾ inches in diameter. Thirty feet above high water, 90 feet above low water, it makes the trip across the chasm in 3½ minutes.

The ferry operates round the clock; the fare is 25 cents per car, 50 cents for a truck, 5 cents for passengers, and free for youngsters.

On up the Fraser

Seven times between Yale and Boston Bar the highway tunnels through the cliffs. Now it continues to wind round the shoulders of the canyon walls all the way to Lytton.

Cedar, fir, balsam, alder, big leaf maple, and graceful vine maple cover the slopes. Autumn turns the scene into a blaze of scarlet and gold.

Clinging to benches cut into either side of the canyon are the tracks of the Canadian Pacific and the Canadian National Railways. At Cisco, each railway crosses to the opposite bank.

Lytton

Lytton is built on a flat bench above the point where the clearer waters of the Thompson mark their passage into the muddy Fraser with a greenish channel. Highway 1 leaves the Fraser at Lytton, and enters the Thompson River Canyon, but a gravel road continues north for 43 miles along the Fraser to Lillooet.

Lillooet

One of the oldest communities in the province, Lillooet originally was Mile 0 on the Cariboo Trail. Opposite Saint Mary's Anglican Church, a monument made of stones from placer diggings marks the start of the gold trail.

The Thompson River Canyon

Now the Trans-Canada Highway heads into the dry belt of the Interior. Slopes that box in the Thompson are rust and ochre, sparsely sprinkled with pines.

Great stretches for steelhead fishing lie along the 23 miles between Lytton and Spences Bridge, particularly below the point where the Nicola River empties into the Thompson.

Numerous campgrounds like Skihist Park, 5 miles east of Lytton, cater to fishermen (70 campsites, a dozen picnic tables, drinking water).

Side trip to Merritt

An hour's drive over Provincial Highway 8 goes from Spences Bridge to Merritt, where the slogan is, "A lake a day as long as you stay."

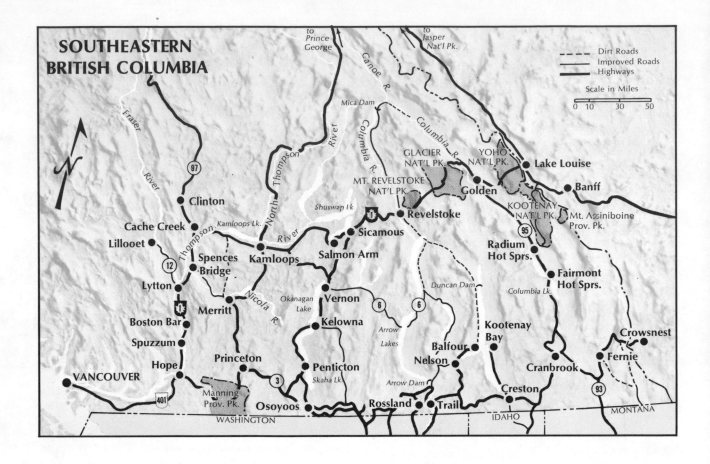

SOUTHEASTERN BRITISH COLUMBIA

Merritt stages a hilarious race on the Nicola River in July in which bathtubs, 45-gallon tanks, and even beer kegs make up the varied craft. An annual rodeo is held over Labor Day.

Land of the Kamloops trout

This region is one of rolling ranch lands, copper mines, and hundreds of small lakes. The Douglas Lake Cattle Ranch 35 miles northeast of Merritt is one of the largest in the Commonwealth. Kamloops trout inhabit almost every lake; steelhead run to 20 pounds in the Nicola River. There's no limit to kokanee in Nicola Lake, and, except for special closures, no closed fishing season in the whole area.

With zero winter temperatures, out come the snowmobiles, the skidoos, and the skis, while fishing continues through the ice of the lakes.

The renowned Kamloops trout is the native rainbow of this country, and for the most part, naturally spawned in the feeder streams of the lakes.

The rainbow trout which Western anglers are used to catching in the United States is generally born and bred in a hatchery. When you catch a fighting 2½ to 3-pound Kamloops on a medium-light tackle, you know the difference.

Rustic lakeshore cabins built of logs are typical fishing camp accommodations. They usually have wood stoves, kerosene lamps, bunks, and water brought by bucket from a central pump. Costs match the facilities: $4 to $10 a night for 4 to 8 persons.

Campgrounds charge $1 to $2 a day. Some lodges supply rooms and meals, and your catch can usually be smoked for 10 cents a fish. Rowboats rent for $2 or $3, motorboats for $5 to $8 a day.

Some American plan dude ranches offer accommodations at rates of $25 to $35 a day for two persons. Write to the Merritt or the Kamloops Tourist Information Centre for a list of accommodations.

Along Highway 1

The Trans-Canada Highway turns east at Cache Creek (where a robber allegedly "cached" his gold). A few miles west of Savona, watch for old apple trees on the sagebrush benchlands off the highway. Here in the valley are remnants of a village built early in this century by the Marquis of Anglesey and a group of British settlers. It is marked on the maps as Walhachin (pronounced Wallasheen).

Orchards were nearly ready to produce when World War I began. Every man volunteered, and all but 10 out of 107 were accepted. Only a handful came back; a cloudburst wrecked the water system, and the entire effort had to be abandoned.

HOUSEBOAT near Sicamous dock is ready for a lake cruising holiday.

At Kamloops the highway intersects the Yellowhead Route. With 10 hotels and 50 motels, Kamloops (population 32,000) has excellent accommodations.

Ten miles east of Kamloops the British Columbia Wildlife Park has a varied collection of more than 100 animals. It is open daily, 9 A.M. to 8 P.M. in summer, 10 A.M. till dusk the rest of the year.

Shuswap Lake

Spreading out like an irregular H, Shuswap Lake consists of a chain of waterways connected by a brief channel known as the Cinnemousun Narrows. Combined, they form nearly 900 miles of shoreline. Resorts are plentiful on the shore of the main lake and on Mara Lake to the south, but much of the northern arms, Seymour and Anstey, are wilderness.

At the narrows, 14 miles north of Sicamous and accessible only by water, is a provincial park designed for vacationers who want their lakes remote. You can rent a boat at Sicamous, or ferry your gear in by barge on a Tuesday or Friday morning. (Ten campsites, 2 cabin shelters, carry drinking water.)

The town of Salmon Arm, on the edge of the lake, is about midway between Vancouver and Calgary, Alberta. A square dance jamboree and a rodeo are part of Salmon Arm's annual July Cherry Festival.

Fishing in Shuswap, noted for Kamloops and lake

HARD WAY DOWN THE FRASER

Simon Fraser thought he was on the Columbia River when he made his unbelievable trip down the Fraser in 1808. He started out in May from Fort George on what Victoria author Bruce Hutchison has called perhaps the "most desperate expedition in the history of western exploration."

Somewhere north of Lytton, the voyageurs had to leave their dugout canoes, but Fraser's goal was to explore the river, and explore it he did. Following the river banks was almost as impossible as running its turbulent rapids.

Above the angry whirlpools of the stream's "black canyon"—now Hell's Gate—the explorers crawled on swaying bark ladders hung against the cliffs, each man with a heavy pack on his back.

Once past Hell's Gate, Fraser was able to use canoes again, and he followed the muddy river to the sea.

Gold was found in the gravel bars of the Fraser in the late 1850's, and by 1861 the Royal Engineers had begun a road, sometimes supported on log stilts above the river, for the hordes of miners.

Now two-lane pavement, the Trans-Canada Highway, climbs easily above it, swinging through tunnels in the rock.

trout, Dolly Vardens, and steelhead, is best in spring and fall. From February through April, fish congregate at the mouth of the Adams River waiting for salmon eggs and fry to drift downstream. Deep trolling is the successful summer method.

Sicamous

Sicamous calls itself the "houseboat capital of Canada." Many Americans spend holidays here cruising Shuswap's varied waterways by houseboat. Four operators rent houseboats at prices ranging from $160 to $295 a week (in-season rentals are by the week, but from mid-September to mid-June you can rent a boat by the day).

Boats vary greatly in size and facilities, but most are fully equipped, with galley sinks, refrigerators, toilets, and lights supplied by 12-volt batteries.

Explicit charts illustrating how to operate and navigate a houseboat are mailed out on receipt of a $50 reservation deposit. Write to the British Columbia Information Center at Sicamous for information (but not for reservations).

Into the mountains

Now Highway 1 climbs gradually into the mountains—the Monashees, the Selkirks, and finally the Rockies.

Yard Creek Park, 8 miles east of Sicamous, has a clear, cold creek flowing through the campground. Good place for a picnic, it has 90 campsites.

Three Valley Gap, 14 miles west of Revelstoke, is a re-created frontier mining town still in the process of being reconstructed board by antique board. Among its Canadiana, it has a 3-story hotel, saloon, barber shop, church dating from 1886, log schoolhouse, blacksmith shop, and a trapper's log hut, each furnished with authentic reminders of a past century.

An old mine train circles the project. The town is open from Easter to November.

Revelstoke is a railway town at the foot of Mount Revelstoke (6,375 feet), accessible by car over a 16-mile gravel road from Revelstoke, open from mid-June to mid-September. The road has many switchbacks but tremendous views, and a picnic area 5 miles up the mountain with shelters, but no campsites. A 9-mile hiking trail on the summit winds through grassy meadows, in summer bright with alpine flowers.

Skiing lasts from December through April on Mount Revelstoke. The annual Tournament of Champions is held during the first week in March.

The Mica Dam

The Mica Dam site, 85 miles north of Revelstoke, may be reached by a paved road up the narrow, scenic Columbia River Valley. The dam is 6 miles from the townsite, Mica Creek. The dam, when completed in 1973, will create an 80-mile-long lake around the Columbia's Big Bend, as well as a 55-mile lake on the Canoe River.

Another 8 miles of gravel road continue north to

BIG SHOW ON A LITTLE RIVER

One of nature's greatest dramas takes place every four years in the Adams and the Little River, that short waterway which connects Little and Big Shuswap Lakes, when as many as 12 million sockeye salmon come home from the sea to spawn and die in the shallow gravel beds of these two streams.

Their backs brilliant scarlet, they turn the water into a seething tide of red. Up from the Pacific through the Fraser's fishways at Hell's Gate, on up the Thompson, and finally into the Adams, the salmon follow a predictable pattern, returning in smaller numbers during the in-between years and in staggering numbers every fourth autumn. The run usually arrives in the Adams shallows around October 20 to 25, and continues for about a week. Peak years of the current decade are 1970, 1974, and 1978.

The spawning beds, which occupy 300 acres of the Little and the Adams Rivers, have been called the "world's richest acres," for this is the greatest known sockeye run in the world.

The sockeye salmon (*Oncorhynchus nerka*) is the most valuable commercial salmon.

The whole saga of the salmon is pure drama. The fry of each year's new hatch—those that are not consumed by hungry trout—spend their first year in Shuswap Lake. As fingerlings, they are no more than 4 inches long when they begin to drift toward the ocean. Four years later, weighing about 7 pounds apiece, they start their return from the sea against fierce river currents, and by the time they find the place of their origin, 300 miles from the sea, they are thin and gaunt. Only when they have entered fresh water do they take on the scarlet color of these last days of their lives.

One excellent place to watch the run is from a platform built over the water on the banks of the Adams River, where you look right down into the mass. Turn off Highway 1 at Squilax. The viewpoint is about 5 miles north.

A lodge and several fishing resorts are nearby, but some close in September, so advance reservations are advisable. Shuswap Lake Provincial Park, 12 miles north of Squilax, offers 269 campsites.

historic Boat Encampment, where the Columbia makes its bend to the south. Here fur traders used to begin their canoe trips downriver.

Mount Revelstoke National Park

This is the first of three national parks on the eastern border of British Columbia traversed by Highway 1 on its 142-mile route between Revelstoke and Lake Louise in Banff National Park, Alberta. Revelstoke Park protects a wilderness among the jagged Selkirks where peaks rise well over 8,000 feet. The highway trails for about 10 miles through their wooded lower slopes along the park's southern margin, then for 11½ miles outside the park follows the Illecillewaet River through its once glacier-filled valley to Glacier National Park.

A $2 license, $3 if you are hauling a trailer, purchased at the entrance to any Canadian national park entitles you to visit all other national and historic parks in Canada. It expires March 31. Just as in the States, no hunting is permitted in any national park.

Glacier National Park

Glacier Park preserves 521 square miles of the ancient Selkirk Mountains, which were formed millions of years before the Rockies. Worthy of its name, the park has more than 100 glaciers, two of which, Asulkan and Illecillewaet, are easily reached by trail. Once called Great Glacier, Illecillewaet is now only 1,000 feet long, and receding at the rate of 50 feet a year.

About a dozen well-marked trails vary from 2 to 12 miles. Many of them start from Illecillewaet Campground, site of once famous Glacier House, built by Canadian Pacific Railway in 1886. To avoid avalanches, rails were re-routed through 5-mile Connaught Tunnel, constructed in 1916, and in 1929 Glacier House was torn down.

Glacier has three campgrounds, Illecillewaet, Loop Creek, and Mountain Creek, the latter with 220 sites. Usually open by July, all have kitchen shelters, piped water, flush toilets, no trailer hookups, and cost $1.50 a night.

Although you look up at gleaming glaciers in nearly every direction, it is difficult under a blue summer sky to imagine winter here when the average snowfall is some 28 feet. Six concrete snowsheds built over the highway remind you of the fact. The sheds allow the snow to slide across their slightly slanting roofs.

To keep the road open the year around, in winter artillery fire is used to persuade threatening avalanches to descend under controlled conditions. Frequent gravel mounds along the highway are also there to break up predictable slides.

Rogers Pass

At 4,354 feet, Highway 1 crosses Rogers Pass. The road climbs nearly 3,000 feet between Revelstoke and the pass, yet the grades make for comfortable 60-mile-per-hour driving. On the level summit are a 60-room motor hotel with dining room (open all year),

ATOP ROGERS PASS, memorial arch honors Major A. B. Rogers, who discovered the pass in 1882.

SHADY CAMP by a trickling stream is in Illecillewaet Campground in Glacier National Park.

a general store, post office, service station, park warden's office, and information center.

Out of the park, the route swings south to Golden, following the eastern arm of the Columbia River through the great Rocky Mountain Trench. At Golden (motel and dining facilities), the jagged Selkirks blot the sky to the west and the Rocky Mountains loom on the eastern horizon.

Yoho National Park

"Yoho" is a Cree Indian exclamation that comes close to matching our "wonderful!" The park's craggy mountains, waterfalls, and lakes are just that. Yoho has 21 peaks higher than 10,000 feet. Generally uncrowded, it has some 200 miles of trails, several alpine lodges, four campgrounds (open July to September).

Both Yoho and adjoining Kootenay National Park to the south push up against the Continental Divide, which is their eastern boundary with Banff National Park and the dividing line between British Columbia and Alberta. Yoho Park headquarters are at Field.

Highway 1 enters Yoho a few miles east of Golden, cuts across the park through the valley of the Kicking Horse River, and crosses the divide via Kicking Horse Pass at an elevation of 5,405 feet.

Fifty miles from Golden, the Trans-Canada Highway intersects the spectacular Jasper-Banff Highway near Lake Louise.

Two hot springs resorts

Highway 95 drops south from Golden to two famous spas, Radium Hot Springs, 67 miles south of Golden, and Fairmont Hot Springs, about 20 miles further south. Each has year-round elegant resorts that feature pools filled with hot mineral waters, and each is a center for winter sports.

Kootenay National Park

From here Highway 93 bisects Kootenay National Park from south to north for 65 miles to the Trans-Canada Highway at Eisenhower Junction in Banff National Park, traveling through Sinclair Pass (4,875 feet) and Vermilion Pass (5,416 feet). The park has six campgrounds and as many picnic areas along the Kootenay River (Redstreak Camp has hookups for 50 trailers.) Black bear are often seen along this route.

The road south

Highway 93-95 continues south along Windermere and Columbia Lakes; the latter is source of the 1,210-mile-long Columbia River. Summer water temperatures average 70° along the lakes' sandy shores. This is David Thompson country; he explored the Columbia River, and erected Kootenae House near Invermere, first trading post on the Columbia, in 1807.

EMERALD LAKE in Yoho National Park is ringed by mountains. You can swim or rent rowboats here.

Helicopter skiing

Thirty miles from Radium Hot Springs, Bugaboo Lodge, operated by Hans Gmoser and Leo Grillmair, has accommodations for 33 persons. From December to May you go in from Spillimacheen by helicopter for a week of fantastic skiing in the ancient Purcell Range. Helicopters take skiers atop a glacier in the morning, drop their lunch at mid-day, pick them up at 6 P.M. Skiing is in groups of 12 behind a guide down untracked slopes. On Bugaboo Glacier you ski approximately 8 miles before reaching the bottom.

THE SOUTHERN TRANS-PROVINCIAL HIGHWAY

Highway 3 skirts British Columbia's southern boundary for 560 miles from Hope to Crowsnest, near the Alberta border. About half of the 83-mile Hope-Princeton section roller coasters south, then north through Manning Provincial Park, 179,000 acres of mountains over 7,000 feet high.

Park features are the Nature House in the Pine Woods administration area midway through the park, nature trails, and conducted walks. Pine Woods Lodge is open all year, and four campgrounds offer nearly 200 sites (no trailer hookups). Rhododendrons are blooming in mid-June.

Monument 83 within the park is the northern terminus for the Pacific Northwest's Pacific Crest Trail.

From the mining village of Princeton, it is 71 miles through the dry Similkameen Valley to Osoyoos on the Washington border. Here Highway 3 turns east, linking the Okanagan country with the Kootenays.

The Okanagan Country

There's no prettier country than the Okanagan, with its long blue lakes, its broad green orchards, and its clean and tree-shaded towns. Miles of warm, sandy beaches, plenty of room for water skiing, acres of parks and golf courses, fine fishing for whopper trout, hot afternoons and cool evenings make the Okanagan a summer playland.

Up through the apple, peach, cherry, and apricot orchards of the Okanagan are numerous lakeshore campgrounds. At Osoyoos, an unusual one is on the spindly spit of land that extends more than half way across Osoyoos Lake. Two miles of the lake are in Washington.

The Okanagan Game Farm, 5 miles south of Penticton, specializes in exotic African animals which wander its 560 hillside acres.

Penticton

Between the southern end of Okanagan Lake and the northern tip of Skaha Lake, Penticton is a town of wide streets, shade trees, parks, and sandy beaches.

Its big yearly celebration, the Penticton Peach Festival, is held Wednesday through Sunday during the first week of August. The festival's most colorful feature is the Square Dance Jamboree held nightly in King's Park; up to 2,500 dancers participate.

Penticton can accommodate 3,000 visitors, but reservations must be made early for festival time.

The old sternwheeler *S.S. Sicamous* houses Penticton's museum. Its Chamber of Commerce information center, open 9 to 5 on weekdays, is in the Jubilee Pavilion, off Martin Street, in the lake front park.

Apex Alpine, 27 miles from Penticton, is the local ski area. At 7,100 feet elevation, Apex is open daily, November to May. Five-day learn-to-ski weeks are featured from January through March.

Kelowna

The Kelowna International Regatta held in early August is this city's biggest annual event. For four days top aquatic stars compete in diving, swimming, water skiing, and sailing. Most performances take place in Aquatic Pool beside Kelowna's pretty lakeside 31½ acre City Park.

Lake-oriented Kelowna is situated near the center of 80-mile-long Okanagan Lake—the community's 17,400 residents claim some 800 boat owners. The City Centre, an attractive complex including the city hall, community theater, courthouse, and federal building, adjoins the park. At the southern end of the long bridge across Okanagan Lake is the Chamber of

WATER SKIERS perform during Kelowna's annual International Regatta on Okanagan Lake.

ON TOUR in the Le Roi Mine, Rossland, visitors don hard hats and hear the guide describe the mining techniques and equipment.

FORT STEELE landmark is giant waterwheel once used in mines.

Commerce information office, open the year around.

Kelowna has many fine accommodations, but motels are often booked a year ahead for regatta days.

Vernon

Apple-growing Vernon has dozens of motel and housekeeping accommodations, many on the shores of Kalamalka and Okanagan Lakes.

Winter brings skiers to Silver Star Mountain, which added a chairlift in 1969, and which features a chalet just for snowmobile buffs. (Rentals are available in the area.) Snowmobile championships are a part of Vernon's gala 10-day Winter Carnival held annually in early February.

The southern stretch

Eastward from Osoyoos Highway 3 climbs grassy slopes, dips into tree-choked arroyos, and runs through small farming villages and old mining settlements. Many parks offer campsites, and modest motel accommodations are available in most towns.

Virtually every community has a travel information booth, a golf course, and a small museum.

The Kootenays

All this country is known as the Kootenays, noted for fishing in summer, hunting in autumn, skiing in win-

ter. Kootenay Lake abounds in kokanee, and in trout to 20 pounds.

Grizzly and black bear are numerous in the West Kootenays, elk in the East, white-tailed deer in both, and there are moose and mountain sheep.

Rossland offers guided tours of a copper mine; at Trail you can tour the Consolidated Mining and Smelting Company plant, largest lead and zinc smelter in the Commonwealth; and at Castlegar you can visit Arrow Dam.

Across the Columbia River from Castlegar are the elegant buildings of Selkirk College on its promontory high above the junction of the Kootenay and the Columbia Rivers. This two-year school is the only Canadian college that offers training for commercial aviation pilots.

Arrow Dam

Nine miles north of Castlegar is 170-foot-high Arrow Dam on the Columbia River. You can drive or walk across it, and perhaps you will be lucky enough to see a boat, or a tug hauling logs through its navigation locks.

This is the second of three British Columbia dams built to regulate the flow of the Columbia. Rising in Columbia Lake south of Kootenay National Park, the river flows north for many miles before making its big bend to the south, circling through southeastern British Columbia for some 480 miles.

Duncan Dam

By taking Highway 3 Alternate from Castlegar through Nelson to Balfour, you can then visit Duncan Dam via a year-round but rather adventurous road that follows along the west side of Kootenay Lake for about 46 miles.

A bonus on this trip is a view of the 2-mile-long spawning channel, where 200,000 kokanee (landlocked salmon) spawn each year beginning in mid-August.

Free ferry ride

A 40-minute ferry ride from Balfour to Kootenay Bay on the eastern shore of Kootenay Lake is claimed to be the "longest free ferry ride on the continent" (nearly six miles). It carries 42 cars, has a coffee counter, and leaves on the hour.

North Star for skiing

The North Star ski area, 2 miles out of Kimberley, on 95-alternate north of Cranbrook, operates daily from mid-November to mid-April. It has lodge, chairlift, two T-bars, one of which is 5,910 feet long, with a vertical drop of 2,000 feet. February's snow fiesta is an annual event in Kimberley.

Fort Steele

At Creston Highway 3 meets the alternate route once more, and continues 67 miles to Cranbrook. About 10 miles east of Cranbrook is re-created Fort Steele, built in 1887, first North West Mounted Police post west of the Rockies.

Fancy fish hatchery

The Kootenay Fish Hatchery on the Bull River southeast of Cranbrook, and about 6 miles north of Wardner, has been called the "Taj Mahal of fish hatcheries." Of contemporary architecture, surrounded by a moat, it is landscaped with modern sculpture, splashing fountains, and flower-bordered walks.

Tanks display fish found in British Columbia waters, and by model, chart, and lighted exhibits, the development of a trout from egg to full grown fish is clearly illustrated.

Admission is free; the hatchery also houses a provincial information center.

Crowsnest Pass

Highway 3 passes through coal mining country, the town of Fernie, and climbs to the summit of 4,580-foot Crowsnest Pass to cross the Rocky Mountains into the province of Alberta.

Soon the broad highway begins to flatten out into the prairies.

POPLAR-LINED ROADS like this are found near the town of Creston in the center of the Kootenays.

INTO THE CARIBOO

Gold lured miners to this country. Fishing and a flavor
of the frontier draw today's visitors

What and where is that special section of British Columbia with the romantic name, The Cariboo? Ask, and you will get half a dozen different answers.

Some insist that the Cariboo is more point of view than place, an easy-paced way of life. But to draw some kind of boundary, start at Cache Creek, go north to Prince George, stretch it out to the mountains both east and west on either side of the Cariboo Highway (97), and you will be inside the Cariboo all the way.

This is a land of rushing waters and yawning canyons, of high, rolling grasslands where white-faced Herefords graze, and of dude ranches and sun-baked communities with one idea—to please the tourist. It is also a land of streams choked by beaver dams, and lakes, and lakes, and lakes.

Gold began the Cariboo as miners plodded north toward Barkerville. The name lured the Overlanders to make an incredible trek westward in 1862, and now it lures travelers for a taste of frontier flavor in a log cabin beside a lake, for rides with cowboys across the rangelands, for western celebrations reminiscent of a hardy past, and for rainbow trout, and Dolly Vardens, and 30-pound lakers.

It is wide open, clean-aired Big Country—rainbows in its waterfalls, sunsets mirrored in its lakes—and once you have met the Cariboo, you understand the magic in the name.

THE CARIBOO HIGHWAY

By 1860, after gold had been found on the sandbars of the Fraser River, thousands of miners were swarming into the interior of British Columbia, a region previously known only to Indians and fur trappers. They could come up from Vancouver as far as Yale by steamer.

The old wagon road

In 1861 the Royal Engineers went to work on a road from Yale through the rugged Fraser River Canyon to the gold fields of Barkerville. It turned out to be the most difficult building project the British Empire had ever tackled. Nevertheless, 300 miles of it had been completed by September, 1863, from Yale to Soda Creek. Here traffic switched again to sternwheelers for the upstream trip to Quesnel.

This was the legendary Cariboo Wagon Road. Over it, mules, oxen, horses, and even camels plodded toward those northern streams that were yielding pure nuggets of gold. Stagecoaches followed.

Now, the Trans-Canada Highway takes you via Hope from Vancouver to Cache Creek, at which point Highway 97, coming west from Kamloops, continues north to Prince George on 60-mile-an-hour, two-lane pavement. This is the Cariboo Highway.

Cariboo loop trip

A delightful loop trip through the center of the Cariboo, and back under the shadow of the Cariboo-Columbia Mountains, may be made by combining the Cariboo Highway to Prince George, the southeast leg of Highway 16 to Jasper, and the Yellowhead Route (Highway 5) south to Kamloops. Start it at Kamloops

RAIL FENCE and deteriorating log cabin of an abandoned homestead on the Dog Creek Road typify the Cariboo back country. Many gravel and dirt roads lead to good fishing lakes.

or at Cache Creek, where the Trans-Canada Highway turns east, and the Cariboo Highway (97) heads north.

You could hurry round it all in two to three days, or spend a summer fishing, canoeing, riding, hiking, and visiting nostalgic gold rush country. Side roads lead to Bowron Lake Provincial Park's chain of lakes, to the grandeur of Mount Robson Provincial Park and Jasper National Park, and to fantastic waterfalls and wilderness camps in Wells Gray Provincial Park.

June into September is the summer season, with hot days in mid-summer, but always cool nights. Remember to bring insect repellent. Early summer's mosquitoes are militant and numerous.

Mile-house towns

Many communities on the Cariboo route are "mile-house" towns that originated as roadhouses on the old Cariboo Wagon Road of gold rush days. Numbered from Lillooet, Mile Zero, they were built about 13 miles apart to keep a fresh team of horses on hand for the stagecoach, and to provide overnight accommodations for passengers. By the time gold mining had declined, some of these stopping places had become centers for a new economy, cattle ranching.

At Cache Creek, the road has already reached an elevation of 1,508 feet on the gradual climb into the plateau country. At Clinton, a cow town 25 miles farther north, it is 2,911 feet. (The South Cariboo Museum here is full of gold rush lore.)

Side roads

All along the highway, gravel roads, often steep and narrow, branch out to places that seem so remote they might be hundreds of miles away. Seven miles north of Cache Creek, Highway 12 goes to Pavilion Lake (rainbow trout to 6 pounds), and the Lillooet region (good hunting here for rockhounds).

A road 11 miles north of Clinton goes east to Loon Lake (excellent rainbow fishing here, too).

Green Lake, an 11-mile stretch cf blue water 8 miles east of the highway, has both rainbows and kokanee (landlocked salmon).

Resorts on Cariboo lakes are rustic, with boat rentals and smokehouses for fishermen, and horses for riders, who may join annual cattle roundups and branding operations.

One offbeat route, the Dog Creek Road, west of 70 Mile House, twists for many miles through the Gang Ranch, one of the continent's huge cattle spreads. Summer fringes the way with wild roses, anemones, black-eyed Susans, and Indian paintbrush.

The road east from 100 Mile House (first gravel,

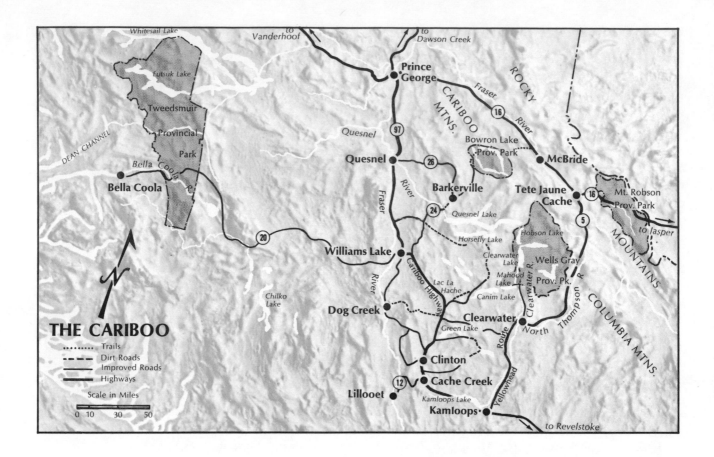

THE CARIBOO

Trails ....
Dirt Roads - - - - -
Improved Roads ——————
Highways ▬▬▬▬▬

Scale in Miles

0 10   30   50

then rough dirt road) threads lake country to Mahood Lake at the rim of Wells Gray Provincial Park.

Lac La Hache

One of the best known lakes in the Cariboo, lying close beside the highway, is Lac La Hache (Lake of the Ax), 15 miles north of 100 Mile House. Eight miles north of the post office, on the east side of the highway across from the lake, is a big government-operated park with 84 campsites.

The 12-mile-long lake has sandy swimming beaches, and good fishing for rainbows and kokanee. The Cariboo Regatta on Lac La Hache each summer is an attractive event featuring water sports and races.

Thirty-two miles north of Lac La Hache, 150 Mile House is the gateway to more finger lakes, like Horsefly Lake (2-pound rainbows, and char to 24 pounds).

A stampede to remember

Early July draws riders and spectators from all over the North American continent to the Williams Lake Stampede. These are seven real frontier days, parades and square dances, whopping breakfasts and bàrbecues, horse racing, with pari-mutuel betting, calf roping, and fierce bronco busting.

Horsemanship is demonstrated at night shows in a big indoor arena in the stampede grounds, right in the middle of town, with some of the world's top cutting horses in competition.

Williams Lake has good motel accommodations, and Scout Island Beach, ½ mile from the stampede grounds, has spaces for tents and trailers. (Make reservations well ahead for Stampede time.)

Every autumn, ranchers drive their cattle to Williams Lake for the huge Cattle Sale. Many come out of the vast Cariboo-Chilcotin country over which Highway 20 winds to distant Bella Coola.

The long road to Bella Coola

In 1793 the Scottish explorer, Alexander Mackenzie, first white man to tackle the Fraser River, managed to get as far as Alexandria via birchbark canoe. Turned back by the Indians' tales of treacherous waters ahead, Mackenzie cached his canoe at the mouth of the Cottonwood River, and took off across the great Chilcotin plateau. *Chilacootin* was the Indian name. On the coast near Bella Coola on the north shore of Dean Channel, with vermilion stirred into melted grease, he painted on a rock: "Alex Mackenzie from Canada by land 22nd July 1793."

Route 20, gravel except for a few miles, winds for

NIMPO LAKE, 198 miles west of Williams Lake on the Bella Coola road, has resorts and boat rentals. This is one of many lakes where you can test your skills against Kamloops trout.

298 miles in lazy loops from Williams Lake to Bella Coola. This is for the slow-paced traveler who likes an offbeat road, and who has no qualms about mountain driving.

Much of it meanders through timbered river valleys; other stretches are semi-arid. At the western end, it goes through the southern half of Tweedsmuir Provincial Park, cuts through a mile-high breach in the coastal mountains, and twists 3,500 feet in 12 miles down into the Bella Coola Valley. Inquire about this section, and don't try to haul a trailer over it. A small camp is at the western edge of the park.

Fly-in lakes are Chilcotin specialties. Rustic lodges have licensed guides and boat rentals, and dude ranches supply a horse for every guest. Check the British Columbia Tourist Directory, and make reservations well ahead.

Bella Coola, busy lumber shipping port, is at the mouth of the Bella Coola River, 75 miles inland.

Ship service. The Northland Navigation Company operates year-around weekly passenger-cargo ship service from here to Vancouver. The *Northland Prince* has air-conditioned, outside stateroom accommodations, with private facilities, for 110 passengers.

Southbound, the ship leaves Bella Coola at 3 P.M. every Sunday, arriving in Vancouver Monday at

BARBECUE is only one of many events scheduled during the annual Williams Lake Stampede in July.

1 P.M. For summer sailings, reservations should be made several months ahead.

Northbound, she leaves Bella Coola Wednesday night, arriving in Prince Rupert on Friday at 8 A.M., then goes on to British Columbia's northernmost port, Stewart, arriving at 8 A.M. Saturday. For more information, write Northland Navigation Company Ltd., 404 Hornby St., Vancouver 111, British Columbia.

Quesnel

Seventy-five miles north of Williams Lake, Quesnel (population, 6,000), has plentiful inn and motor court accommodations. The town, named for Simon Fraser's lieutenant, Maurice Quesnelle, is situated where the Quesnel River joins the Fraser.

An attractive museum adjoining the information center (open 8:30 A.M. to 8 P.M., May 1 to October 15) exhibits memorabilia of gold rush days.

To Barkerville

A spur road goes east from Quesnel to Wells and Barkerville (56 miles), once the end of the line for the miners on the Cariboo Wagon Road. It goes past historic spots like Cottonwood House, a roadhouse built in 1864 that is being restored.

Bowron Lake Provincial Park

A few miles beyond Barkerville is the entrance to Bowron Lake Provincial Park, with a chain of lakes that nature appears to have designed especially for canoeists. Six major lakes and smaller waterways form an almost rectangular border within the park, stretching for 73 miles. The trip around the chain by canoe takes a good 10 days (storms may slow the pace), and requires both a sturdy canoe and canoeist. Seven portages are involved in making the circuit. (Lots of moose here, but no hunting.) Two lodges on Bowron Lake near the park entrance furnish accommodations, meals, boats, and guides. Lakeshore campsites are located at designated points.

Prince George

Prince George (population approximately 28,000) has become one of Canada's fastest growing cities. Pulp

BILLY BARKER'S HOLE IN THE GROUND

When Billy Barker had sunk his shaft 40 feet into the mud beside Williams Creek, the miners who were taking gold out of the hills beyond said that he was crazy. But Barker, a stubborn Cornish sailor, went on digging, and in another two feet he hit the most fantastic pay dirt in the Cariboo.

Downhill came the miners. Up went the log

BOISTEROUS BARKERVILLE had its Sunday side. This is Canadian Anglican Church.

shacks round his shaft, a town sprouted, and the miners named it Barkerville. For awhile it was said to be the largest city west of Chicago and north of San Francisco, and during its comparatively brief boom, some $50 million in gold were taken out of the streams and slopes nearby.

Billy Barker dug out a fortune that amounted to about $1,000 for every foot of the 600-foot strip which he mined—and he died without a sou in an old man's home in Victoria.

When the boom town burned to the ground in 1868, it was immediately rebuilt, but when the gold began to peter out, Barkerville's saloons and hotels, its blacksmith shop and assay office were deserted. It was a real ghost town until 1958 when the British Columbia Provincial Government began its restoration.

The restored town has as nearly as possible the authentic look of those pick and shovel days of the 1860's. There is Kelly's Saloon, the barber shop, Barker's own mine shaft, while in a fine, up-to-date museum, open from June to September, you can learn just how gold was mined here a century ago.

In Barkerville's heyday, thespians gave performances of Shakespeare in the Theatre Royal, and were paid in gold nuggets. Now from mid-June until September, a vaudeville show is presented twice a day at the theater.

and paper production top its economy. Tours may be taken to such plants as the Kraft mill of Prince George Pulp and Paper, Ltd.

Simon Fraser built a post (Fort George) here at the mouth of the Nechako River in 1807. Now bank buildings, apartment houses, and hotels like the Inn of the North stretch the city's profile skyward. The city is the crossroads for travel between the populous south and the "far North".

See Connaught Hill Park, and the contemporary sculpture and mural at the Centennial Fountain.

Mount Taber ski area. Eight to 10 feet of powder snow provides great skiing on Mount Taber, 13 miles east of the city via Highway 16. Its five beginning-to-expert runs vary in length from 3,200 to 6,000 feet.

Mount Taber operates Friday through Monday, Wednesdays and holidays, 9 A.M. to 4 P.M., from November to April. There's night skiing from 7 to 10 on Fridays and Saturdays. The resort has a day lodge with dining room, cafeteria, and ski shop, and there's bus service from Prince George.

Prince George stages an annual winter carnival, with exciting races at Mount Taber in March, and a figure skating show in April.

PRINCE GEORGE TO JASPER

The 216 miles of Highway 16 along the upper Fraser River from Prince George to Jasper National Park are scenic all the way. This section of highway alone, completed in 1969, cost $30 million. It makes 19 major crossings over the Fraser and its tributaries. Although sometimes 137 inches of snow falls in Red Pass, the first of two passes through the Rockies, this is year-around, all-weather road.

On the outskirts of McBride, Oscar's Museum has stuffed lynx, mountain goats, cougar, and beaver, and trophy heads of moose and caribou. Also on display is a good rock collection.

McBride has a small hotel; there's a motor village on the highway near the boundary of Mount Robson Provincial Park, and a dude ranch on the road to Robson Station. The park offers 21 campsites beside Robson River and 29 at the Lucerne camp on Yellowhead Lake. (Carry drinking water.)

The highway climbs easily over Yellowhead Pass,

QUESNEL stock auction brings annual cattle drives from the big Cariboo and Chilcotin ranches.

PRINCE GEORGE is main crossroads connecting the coast with Alberta, the Cariboo with far North.

at 3,760 feet, lowest cut through the Canadian Rockies, as it swings below the range's highest peak, Mount Robson (12,972 feet). Jasper is 65 miles east of Tete Jaune Cache.

THE YELLOWHEAD ROUTE

Sixty-five miles west of Jasper, the Yellowhead Route, Highway 5, veers south from Highway 16 at Tete Jaune Cache. Tete Jaune, French for Yellow Head, was the nickname given a fair-haired fur trapper. Most localities run it together, and say "Teezhon."

The road and the Canadian National Railway both follow the North Thompson River. Within 25 miles of Mount Robson Provincial Park, you drive through three watersheds, the Fraser, the Canoe which flows into the Columbia, and the North Thompson.

Since this is comparatively new highway, campgrounds and overnight stopping places are scarce, but you'll find numerous attractive picnic spots along the way.

Wells Gray Provincial Park

The Yellowhead road enables you to visit Wells Gray Provincial Park, some 1,300,000 acres of wilderness cut through by five major lakes, two large rivers, many smaller waterways, and impressive waterfalls.

A gravel road leads north from Clearwater 25 miles to the park entrance and headquarters at Hemp Creek.

MAJESTIC MOUNT ROBSON towers above Highway 16, usually has its head in the clouds.

Off the 21-mile dirt road within the park which goes to Clearwater Lake, you discover both Dawson Falls, a 300-foot-wide Niagara-like cascade in the Murtle River, and a few miles downstream, spectacular Helmcken Falls.

July through September is the best time to visit the park, but go prepared for mosquitoes, and for possible thunder showers. You may see black bear anywhere, grizzlies and goats in the northern mountains, moose in the southern and western sections.

Trails go to flower-filled alpine meadows. Canoes and outboard motorboats may be rented at Clearwater Lake, and a 64-mile roundtrip on Clearwater and Azure Lakes is a park feature. Before taking off by boat or on foot, however, check with the park staff, or hire a park guide.

There are some 50 campsites in the park at Dawson Falls, 5 miles north of the park entrance at Clearwater Lake, and at Mahood Lake, the latter only accessible from the west. Accommodations outside the park are available at resorts near Clearwater.

The Overlanders

The Overlanders, headed for Barkerville, came this way along the North Thompson in 1862. After trekking across the Yellowhead Pass from the prairies of Alberta, they divided. One group went down the Fraser River, and was never heard from again. The other struggled through the dense forest beside the North Thompson River, finally arriving at Fort Kamloops. Out of 150 persons who left Edmonton, fewer than 20 made it.

Kamloops

Kamloops celebrates their arrival every year during the third week in July with its Kami-Overlander Days, when beards and 19th century costumes are the fashion. Raft and canoe races on the Thompson are exciting events among festivities.

You can fish for those outsize Kamloops trout from May to October, go after them again through holes in the ice all winter, and ski from December into April. Swimming in the lakes and rivers is also fine during warm summer days.

Ski area. Tod Mountain, 33 miles northeast of Kamloops, is open daily, 9 A.M. to 4:30 P.M., from December 1 to Easter. Nearby Grandview Ski Acres and Lac Le Jeune have skiing and tobogganing.

Back to Cache Creek

Kamloops Lake, a 3-mile-wide bulge in the Thompson River, stretches for 28 miles beside the highway to west of Savona. With trout to five pounds, fishing is particularly good here in spring. There are campsites at Savona.

FISHERMEN prepare their tackle for a morning's outing on Salmon Lake. You reach the lake by gravel road from either Kamloops or Merritt. This is the heart of Kamloops trout country.

THE NORTHLAND

Wildlife abounds in this big country. From here
you take off for Alaska or sail down the Inside Passage

Prince George not only connects with Edmonton, Alberta, via two through highways—southeast across Yellowhead Pass and northeast by the John Hart Highway—but it opens up the whole vast northern region of the province. Trans-Provincial Highway 16 swings northwest to the southern tip of Alaska; while northwest from Dawson Creek the Alaska Highway, shoved through miles of muskeg during World War II as a supply route to Alaska, crosses 620 miles of this British Columbia northland.

Up here, summer days are 20 hours long, but from mid-November to mid-March, this is a cold and silent land. Here trappers still live with their sled dogs on remote lake shores, moose graze in the marshes, and Dall sheep climb the craggy mountains.

The Hart Highway also gives access to the rolling wheat fields of the Peace River District to the northeast. This Great Plains Region of the North American continent is rightly called the "Bread Basket of British Columbia."

FROM PRINCE TO PRINCE

The northwestern leg of Trans-Provincial Highway 16 connecting Prince George and Prince Rupert is a water level route for all its 455 miles, lowest road through the Coast Mountains. Because of this link, it is possible to make a wonderful land-sea loop trip via the Cariboo Highway through central British Columbia, and by auto-ferry cruise on the Inside Passage between Prince Rupert and Kelsey Bay.

Vanderhoof

The first 62 miles from Prince George to Vanderhoof are typical of the country—rolling hills densely covered with spruce, fir, western red cedar, and lodgepole pine (locally called bull pine).

Curiously, Vanderhoof was named for a Chicago publisher, Herbert Vanderhoof, who dreamed of developing an ideal place of retirement for writers. Instead, like other communities that grew after the railroad came, Vanderhoof became a lumber town.

Fort St. James

Forty-one miles north of Vanderhoof, Fort St. James at the southern tip of Stuart Lake is the takeoff point for that 75-mile-long waterway of the Fraser River system which includes Stuart, Trembleur, and Takla Lakes. These are usually open from mid-May to freezeup in late October (rainbow trout to 15 pounds, lakers to 30 pounds).

Guides use extra long, sturdy boats on these often wind-churned waters. From late August into December, this is also outstanding moose-hunting country.

Fort St. James has a long history. Simon Fraser established it in 1806 as capital of the fur-trading region he named New Caledonia.

Burns Lake

Roads branch north from the community of Burns Lake, 80 miles beyond Vanderhoof, to renowned

SEAPLANE lands on Stuart Lake at old Fort St. James, northwest of Prince George. Charter flights to fly-in lakes of British Columbia are popular with many avid fishermen.

Babine Lake, British Columbia's largest lake, 110 miles long. Babine drains into the Skeena River system (cutthroats, rainbows, and 35-pound char here). Trolling is good from June, and fly fishing particularly good in late May and early June when the fish congregate to feed on young sockeye salmon that appear from tributary streams.

Autumn draws steelhead and chinook enthusiasts to such rivers as the Babine, the Copper, the Skeena, and the Kispiox, where a world-record 36-pound steelhead was caught.

Burns Lake is also the gateway to some 2 million acres of wilderness in Tweedsmuir Provincial Park, 40 miles to the south. From the small settlements, Ootsa Lake and Wistaria, accessible by gravel road and free ferry south of Burns Lake, guided boat trips trace a nearly 300-mile network of waterways that stretches like a moat around the little-visited park. Experienced guides are needed for these sometimes dangerous waters.

Leaping salmon

If you are here during August and September, stop at the Moricetown Fishways opposite the Indian village of Moricetown, 22 miles north of Smithers. Here the once placid Bulkley River squeezes into a narrow cataract so turbulent that homecoming salmon often cannot make it. Many salmon use the fishways, but others struggle to leap the falls, where Indians, following ancient tradition, spear them.

'Ksan

An authentic and charming Indian village, a replica of a Gitskan community which stood on the same site when the first fur traders came to the area, is at Hazelton, 4 miles north of New Hazelton. It could hardly have a more striking setting, situated as it is almost on an island encircled by the Skeena River ('Ksan means Skeena in the regional Indian language) and the Bulkley River, with the Rocher Deboule Range standing high and white as backdrop.

The Skeena Treasure House. Formerly a museum built in the manner of an Indian communal house, this building was moved to serve as the nucleus of a "Worker's House," one of four long houses constructed after the fashion of such Indian structures.

Indian craftsmen work here at carving and painting, bead and leather work, and training programs are underway to preserve these ancient skills. Articles, each with the 'Ksan trademark, the "Indian hand of history," may be purchased here.

Indian village. Totem poles stand tall in the re-created village, each telling its own story and bearing the family crest. Canoes are on display, and even fish traps and smokehouses.

Each of the four long houses illustrates a facet of early Indian life. One, the "Stone Age House," dates back to the days of cedar bark culture, when almost everything in the way of clothing and utensils was made of bark. Another, the "Feast House," shows

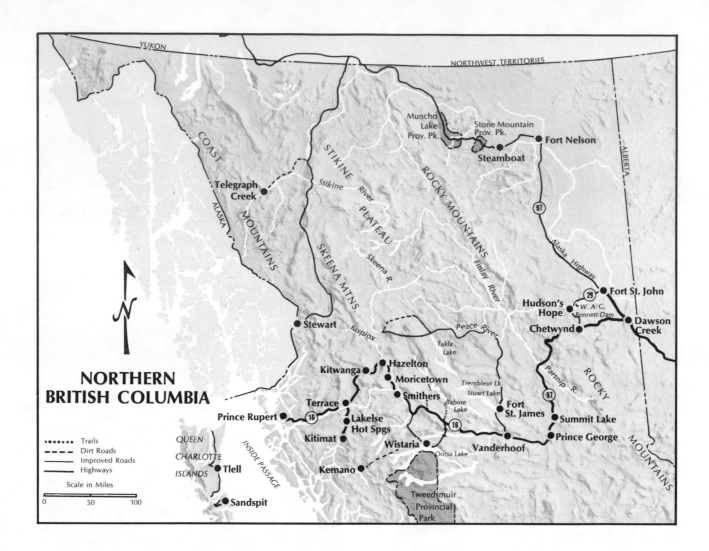

NORTHERN BRITISH COLUMBIA

Trails
Dirt Roads
Improved Roads
Highways

Scale in Miles

0   50   100

how the Gitskan tribe lived in the days after white men arrived.

The 'Ksan project was brought about through the joint efforts of the 'Ksan Association and the Canadian and British Columbia Governments.

Campground. Local Indians operate a campground, constructed by the Provincial Parks Branch, near 'Ksan Village. It has about 40 tent and trailer sites, as well as picnicking areas.

More totems

If you want to see more fine examples of totem poles, almost a dozen superbly carved poles reach skyward at Kispiox, 12 miles north of Hazelton by a gravel road, and there are more poles at Kitwanga on the northern side of the Skeena.

Along the Skeena

From New Hazelton, Highway 16 follows the Skeena, where, in the 1890's, men cruised upriver on steam-operated sternwheelers, and gold was freighted downstream. The 9,000-foot peaks of the Seven Sisters rise above this scenic section of road.

Kitimat

Kitimat, where the third largest aluminum smelter on the North American continent is located, is easily reached by paved road south of Terrace. On the Douglas Channel 80 miles inland from the Pacific, this community now has a population of nearly 10,000.

To get there, turn south onto Highway 25 at its junction with Highway 16, 5 miles east of Terrace. Kitimat is 37 miles south.

Alcan plant tours. Daily weekday tours are offered through the huge Aluminum Company of Canada (Alcan) plant. A fantastic project developed at the edge of this deep water blue bay at the foot of densely forested mountains of the Coast Range, the Alcan plant has the capacity to produce 236,000 tons of aluminum ingots annually.

To generate the electric power needed, the Nechako River, tributary to the Fraser, was checked by the huge Kenny Dam west of Vanderhoof to create a 358-square mile reservoir. From this, water is diverted through a 10-mile-long tunnel, and dropped 2,600 feet from the tunnel to turbines in the Kemano powerhouse built deep within a mountain south of Kitimat.

The power produced at Kemano is delivered by a 51-mile transmission line over mile-high Kildala Pass to the Kitimat smelter.

Bauxite from Jamaica is unloaded at Kitimat's 750-foot-long wharf, and fluorspar comes from the mines of Newfoundland to be used in the manufacture of aluminum ingots.

Tours of the smelter leave daily, Monday through Friday, at 9 and 10:30 A.M. and 1 and 3 P.M. You should reserve space in advance either by writing or by telephoning Kitimat 620. Pre-school-age children are not permitted on the tour.

Lakelse. Hot mineral water swimming pools are featured at the resort at Lakelse, 12 miles south of the junction of Highways 16 and 25.

Lakelse Lake Park, provincial campground on Furlong Bay, provides 31 campsites and 45 picnic tables. This lake is one place the rare trumpeter swan may be found.

Prince Rupert

In Chatham Sound, only about 20 miles south of Alaska, Prince Rupert is often called the "Halibut Capital of the World." Fascinating to watch is the unloading of halibut, herring, cod, sole, and in autumn, salmon.

Five cold storage plants, one said to be the largest in the world, store the fish. Seven canneries process it. You may see the whole process, and even visit the huge cold storage plant if you don't mind a few minutes in temperatures down to −30°.

Tours through the Columbia Cellulose Company pulp mill are also available.

Inquire about these and about the harbor cruises and trips by sea plane to Port Simpson, oldest settlement on the British Columbia coast, at the Tourist Bureau in the Centennial Museum, McBride and 1st Avenue, beside the Courthouse grounds.

Arts of the Haida Indians of the Queen Charlotte Islands, across Hecate Strait from Prince Rupert, are on exhibit in this attractive modern museum. Among the most interesting collections are the unique Haida totems made of argillite.

From Prince Rupert, Alaska State Ferries go through and to the top of the Inside Passage, and British Columbia Ferries connect with Kelsey Bay on Vancouver Island.

FREIGHTERS dock beside the grain elevator in Prince Rupert's large natural harbor, ice-free all year.

ALUMINUM INGOTS being loaded on freighter at Kitimat's Alcan plant are headed for world markets.

UNLOADING HALIBUT from commercial fishing fleet, Prince Rupert. Cold storage plants flank docks.

MOOSE is the prize of the northland. Non-resident hunters must hunt with a licensed guide.

Wildlife

Sportsmen know this part of British Columbia for its long chain lakes, for its salmon and steelhead streams, and for its big game—trophy moose, goats, caribou, bears, and deer. You are likely to see as many moose in this region as anywhere in the province. As you drive highway 16, watch for golden eagles. The Vanderhoof area is a major flyway for Canadian geese, swans, and other migratory fowl.

A surprising number of motel and hotel accommodations are available in towns along the highway, and many hunting and fishing lodges and government-operated camps are located back on the lakeshores.

Canadian National Railway and Canadian Coachways serve this area. From the main communities like Vanderhoof, Burns Lake, and Smithers, charter flights may be arranged to remote lakes with such lines as Northern Mountain Airlines, Omineca Airways, and Alpine Helicopters, Ltd. Licensed guides are available throughout the region. See the listing in the back of the British Columbia Tourist Directory, or contact any Chamber of Commerce along the highway.

THE JOHN HART HIGHWAY

Provincial Highway 97 continues northeast for 256 miles from Prince George to Dawson Creek as the John Hart Highway. Angling through the Rocky Mountains in a section locally called the Murray Range, it is one of British Columbia's most scenic roads. It crosses many streams, borders peaceful lakes, and once on the eastern side of the mountains, traverses the fertile fields of the Peace River District.

Two provincial campgrounds close to the highway, one at Bear Lake, 45 miles north of Prince George, another at McLeod Lake, another 41 miles north, both have sandy beaches pleasant for swimming. Communities along the route offer plenty of good accommodations.

Waters drain north

After Summit Lake, 30 miles north of Prince George, the waterways all flow "down north" toward the Arctic Ocean. Arctic grayling are a favorite with fly fishermen here. Although seldom more than 18 inches long, the grayling is a game fighter. Summer anglers try for them in the Parsnip River and in Tudyah Lake, north of McLeod Lake.

A great dam on the Peace River

At Chetwynd, a paved road branching north, Provincial Highway 29, goes for 54 miles to the W. A. C. Bennett Dam, one of the world's great power projects. Six hundred feet high, 1¼ miles long, and a half mile wide at its base, it is one of the largest earth-filled dams in existence.

Carved out of bedrock 500 feet below the eastern shoulder of the dam is the 890-foot-long Gordon M. Shrum generating station.

The great reservoir formed behind the structure, Ray Williston Lake, eventually will be 225 miles long, with a shoreline of 1,100 miles. Begun in 1962, the first power was produced here in the fall of 1968.

Visitors viewing the complex from the top floor reception center are likely to feel as awed as Sir Alexander Mackenzie himself who, when he first saw the Peace River Canyon in 1793, called it "awful to behold."

Two high speed elevators at the center give access to the powerhouse below.

THE LONG, LONG ROAD TO ALASKA

The 1,523-mile drive from Mile 0, Dawson Creek, to Fairbanks, Alaska, is a special sort of adventure, but only for the traveler long on patience, and willing to put up with such nuisances as dust and mosquitoes. All but 300 miles of the route is in Canada. The trip can be made easily in a week or less, but this leaves little time for enjoying the mountain scenery, the

---

THE WILD STIKINE

Every six days between May 16 and September 22, a sturdy little ship, the *Margaret Rose*, pushes into northern British Columbia on one of the world's wildest rivers, the Stikine. This is one of a very few such river boat rides still available on the North American continent, and those who have discovered it come again and again for the superb 4-day roundtrip cruise that begins at Wrangell, Alaska.

The 65-foot-long vessel, three decks tall, ties up each night in mid-stream, often to a huge pile of driftwood, to escape the on-shore mosquitoes. You need miss none of the dramatic mountains, glaciers, or waterfalls along the way.

The Stikine rises high in the Cassiar Mountains, winds northwest, finally bends south for its headlong dash to salt water near Wrangell. The *Margaret Rose* chugs upstream to Telegraph Creek, as far as the fast water is navigable. This small settlement of Tahltan Indians is takeoff point for hunters heading into the Cassiars after sheep.

Although mail comes to Telegraph Creek by air now, the small ship still carries supplies, particularly to the "snagger" camps. By treaty between Canada and the United States, the Stikine is kept open from thaw to freezeup, which requires a continuing battle against snags and logjams.

The scenery is dramatic, but the cruise is easy-paced. Where sternwheelers churned upstream in the 1890's during the Klondike gold rush, the *Margaret Rose* plows along at about four knots an hour, an ideal rate for camera fans.

In the approximately 350-mile roundtrip, she climbs well over 500 feet in the upriver voyage of 2½ to 3 days, skimming downstream in a day.

The *Margaret Rose* has 13 spare but comfortable staterooms, each with two berths, and hot and cold water. Showers and toilets are down the passageway. Meals are hearty, with salmon, crab, or fresh trout featured on most menus.

Reservations for the cruise ($185 per person) must be made well in advance with the Stikine Transportation Company, Wrangell, Alaska 99929.

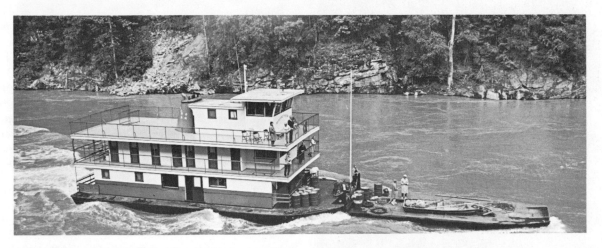

THE "MARGARET ROSE" bucks tremendously powerful currents as it navigates Little Canyon on the Stikine River. Four-day cruise passes through relatively untouched country.

fishing streams, the old trading posts, and the moose, bear, and even bison you see along the way.

When to go

The highway is open all year except for temporary winter closures. Most people drive it between early June and mid-August, but from mid-August to mid-October is perhaps the most pleasant time. Days are cool then, traffic sparse, and summer pests like mosquitoes, "no-see-ums," and deer flies are mostly gone. Also birch and aspen weave patterns of gold in the forests. But be prepared with warm clothing, tire chains, shovel, and tow rope for possible snow.

There are no bad grades, however, and the road is well maintained, gravel all the way through Canada after the first 85 miles of pavement, and pavement again from the Alaskan border to Fairbanks. Service stations are generally 25 to 50 miles apart.

Where to stop

Both Dawson Creek and Fort St. John have excellent accommodations. Those along the rest of the highway

ALASKA HIGHWAY is well-maintained gravel most of the way; late summer into fall is best driving time.

are considerably rustic, possibly crowded and a little higher priced in summer. Four government campgrounds are located along British Columbia's 620-mile section of the road, one of them, at Mile 493, featuring hot springs.

From Mile 0: It is 300 miles from Dawson Creek to Fort Nelson (old Hudson's Bay post nearby), another 618 miles to Whitehorse, Yukon, and 91 more to Haines Junction, from which a 135-mile road branches south to Haines, connecting with the Alaska Ferry system there.

You can, of course, make one leg of the trip to Alaska by Alaskan ferry on the Inside Passage. At Skagway, you might even take the narrow-gauge railroad across White Pass to Whitehorse, hauling the car along on a flatcar. (Car and two passengers cost $65 one way.)

Customs. You reach Canadian Customs at Mile 1202 (there's a 62-room lodge here), and U.S. Customs in another 112 miles at Tok Junction. From here it is 209 more miles to Fairbanks.

THE INSIDE PASSAGE

British Columbia's "Marine Highway," the fabulous Inside Passage to Alaska, has become one of the most popular trips in the Northwest. Many cruise ships to Alaska now ply these "inside" waters between the British Columbia mainland and the coast's long string of offshore islands.

Ferry Service

A real boon to motorists who want to sample northern British Columbia and Alaska without driving the long roundtrip is the ferry service between Kelsey Bay on the northern end of Vancouver Island and Prince Rupert.

British Columbia Ferries' *Queen of Prince Rupert* carries 430 passengers and 90 automobiles on the 330-mile voyage. The non-stop, overnight cruise takes 20 hours.

Leaving Kelsey Bay at 1:30 P.M., the 325-foot motor vessel pulls into Prince Rupert's beautiful, natural harbor the next morning at 9:30. Sailing south, she leaves Prince Rupert at 12:30 P.M., arriving at the little lumber community of Kelsey Bay at about 8:00 A.M. the next day, depending on tide conditions.

All summer the *Queen of Prince Rupert* sails north and south on alternate days. During winter, northbound cruises leave on Tuesdays and Thursdays, southbound on Wednesdays and Saturdays. You may park your car near the ticket office at Kelsey Bay if you want to make the roundtrip cruise without it. You will have three hours in the northern port between sailings.

The cruise. As the ferry heads north from Kelsey Bay, she hugs the shore of Vancouver Island, then cuts across Queen Charlotte Sound to the shelter of Calvert and Hunter Islands, for protection from the wind and waves of the Pacific.

The Inside Passage is more like river than ocean; only in three places—Queen Charlotte Sound, Milbanke Sound, and Dixon Entrance—do you sail on open sea. Through island-dotted fiords you voyage past a wilderness of densely forested mountains.

Shipboard accommodations. Staterooms are small but adequate. The ferry has several lounges located fore and aft, a dining room, cafeteria, and a souvenir and magazine stand (no bar).

Fare is $30 per passenger one way, half fare for children 5 to 11 years old, with a 10 per cent reduction for the roundtrip.

Automobiles, including driver, cost $60 one way, $114 both ways. Mobile homes and campers up to 20 feet long cost $75, $144 for the roundtrip, including driver. The cost of taking a boat trailer is figured at $3.60 per foot.

Stateroom costs range from 4-berth setups, with public bathroom facilities, at $18 per unit, to 2-berth cabins with shower and bathroom at $11.50 for each berth. Fares are 25 per cent lower between mid-September and mid-May.

For further information and reservations, write British Columbia Ferries, P.O. Box 1388, Victoria, British Columbia, Canada.

Making connections

Kelsey Bay. If you plan to drive up Vancouver Island the 220 miles from Victoria to catch the ferry, leave the capital at 8 A.M.

Or if you prefer to go by bus, the Vancouver Island Coach Lines bus leaves Victoria at 7:45 A.M. to connect with the afternoon sailing. Fare is $12.80 one way.

Prince Rupert. Alaska State Ferries, ships that can carry 500 passengers and 108 autos, make connections with the British Columbia ferry at Prince Rupert. They offer service six days a week in summer, four days each week in winter, to Ketchikan, Wrangell, Petersburg, Sitka, Juneau, Haines, and Skagway, Alaska.

THE QUEEN OF PRINCE RUPERT leaves Kelsey Bay, Vancouver Island, on regular voyages to Prince Rupert. From here, connections can be made with the Alaska ferry.

ALBERTA

Buffalo by the millions ranged the prairies when, half a century before Lewis and Clark crossed the Rocky Mountains to the Pacific Ocean, Anthony Henday became the first white man to break trail in Alberta. He came in 1754 on a futile effort for Hudson's Bay Company to persuade the Indians to provide furs for eastern markets.

In 1793 Sir Alexander Mackenzie traveled up the Peace River by canoe, and on across country to the "western sea". Another early explorer, David Thompson, tried first to cross the Canadian Rockies in 1802; he succeeded on another try in 1807, and went on to find the mouth of the Columbia River.

Hudson's Bay and North West Companies were rivals for the fur trade; in 1821 they were consolidated under the Hudson's Bay firm. After the fur brigades came the gold seekers, the Overlanders in 1862, and the mob that answered the call to the Klondike in 1897 and '98.

Hudson's Bay Company holdings were transferred to Canada in 1869, leaving no one in charge on the plains—home of Blackfoot, Blood, Peigan, Stony, Cree, and other Indian tribes.

Americans helped brew the trouble that ensued, scorning to pay customs duties, and some of them preferring the quick profits of the illicit whisky trade. So Ottawa sent out the first North-West Mounted Police (now Royal Canadian Mounted Police) in 1874 to bring order to the area.

Alberta became a district in 1882, and a province in 1905. Soon after this, the first discoveries of oil

and natural gas were made, the beginning of an era which continues in the growth of Alberta's beautiful and cosmopolitan cities.

The province of Alberta covers more than a quarter-million square miles, reaching from the Montana border to the North West Territories and from the spine of the Canadian Rockies, British Columbia boundary, to the province of Saskatchewan.

Jasper and Banff National Parks extend along the eastern side of the Continental Divide. Here snow-capped peaks line the horizon; magnificent mountain scenery and a wide variety of outdoor activities draw more than 2 million visitors a year. The two parks are connected by the Columbia Icefield Highway, which passes near snow and ice remaining from the Ice Age.

The grain-rich prairies stretch eastward from the Rockies like a golden sea. In every community, huge grain storage towers line the railroad tracks. The southern plains, 2,000 feet and more above sea level, merge northward into rolling hills, and finally into stunted woodland and sub-Arctic tundra. Dinosaurs once roamed this area, which today is Canada's oil capital and home of the Athabasca Oil Sands, still the largest known oil reserve in the world.

In this vast area, more than 1,500,000 people reside, most of them in the south-central portion of the province, with another populous section in the northwestern wheat lands of the Peace River Valley.

Alberta's climate varies with its great distances, but in general is characterized by dry, hot summers, and dry, cold winters. Winter temperatures average from a low of $-19°$ in the north to $2°$ in the south, where warm winds often come up suddenly to melt away, overnight, a fall of snow.

ICEFIELD HIGHWAY skirts mountains from Lake Louise to Jasper. Mount Athabasca in background.

ALBERTA'S NATIONAL PARKS

Banff…Jasper…Waterton Lakes…Elk Island…Wood Buffalo

Nine of Canada's 19 national parks are in Western Canada, four in British Columbia, and five in Alberta. In Alberta's southwestern corner, the national sanctuary that surrounds Waterton Lakes combines with Glacier National Park in Montana to form an international park.

Elk Island National Park is a small one in the center of the Alberta prairies, and huge Wood Buffalo Park in the forest and tundra of the north is a great national game preserve, but without tourist facilities.

The Continental Divide not only forms the boundary between Alberta and British Columbia, it marks the division between several national parks. Much of Banff Park on the east side of the Rockies adjoins Kootenay and Yoho on the west side, while Jasper, farther north, abuts British Columbia's Mount Robson Provincial Park and Hamber Provincial Park.

Nowhere has nature been more lavish with its mountainscapes than along this northern roof of the continent. Peak after peak reaches for the sky, again and again topping the 10,000-foot, sometimes the 11,000-foot level, while on the western edge of the Divide, Mount Robson tops them all at 12,972 feet. Mount Columbia, highest point in Alberta, comes close with 12,294 feet.

The dividing line between Alberta's contiguous parks, Banff and Jasper, is near the southern edge of the Columbia Icefield, which occupies part of each of the parks.

These national preserves atop the Canadian Rockies attract around 2 million visitors a year, both for summer holidays and winter sports. Banff has usually drawn the largest number. The town of Banff, on Trans-Canada Highway 1, is only 85 miles east of Golden (where Highways 1 and 95 intersect), 81 miles west of Calgary, and 83 miles northeast of Radium Hot Springs in Kootenay National Park via Highway 93. Its permanent population is around 3,600 persons, but it is estimated that about ten times that number are in town on an average day in midsummer.

Jasper Park has usually been pleasantly less crowded than Banff and Lake Louise. The travel pattern is changing, however, now that the new Yellowhead Route from Kamloops (Highway 5) has made this road the most direct link between Edmonton and Vancouver, putting Jasper on a main tourist east-west thoroughfare.

The Jasper-Banff Highway is an extension of number 93 north from Lake Louise. Called the Columbia Icefield Highway, it connects the two parks and is one of the world's great high roads. Along it, glaciers almost nudge the broad pavement. Streams milky with glacial silt flow beside it, and cold lakes, dotted with tiny fir and spruce-tufted islands, reflect the towering shapes of the mountains.

Along the highway, glaciers almost nudge the broad pavement. Streams milky with glacial silt flow along beside it, and cold lakes, dotted with tiny fir and spruce-tufted islands, reflect the towering shapes of the surrounding mountains.

Numerous campgrounds and picnic areas line the highway, and there are many roadside turnouts for travelers who wish to stop for a longer look.

SKYLINE TRAIL HIKERS enjoy the spectacular mountain scenery of the Canadian Rockies in Banff National Park. Hikers can choose from many long or short hikes in the region.

Renowned hotels in both parks, along with elegant newer ones, offer luxury in the mountains. Lodges, motels, and cabins are numerous, and campgrounds plentiful. All commercial accommodations are inspected by the national park service. On request, the Canadian Government Travel Bureau, 165 Kent Street, Ottawa, will send its free book of accommodations for all of Canada's national parks. It is a good thing to have so that you can write ahead for reservations during the heavy part of the tourist season, July and August. The booklet also lists details about park campgrounds.

The parks have an extensive program to help visitors enjoy their stay and understand the park. Naturalists conduct interpretive programs on plant and animal life, land formations, and climate. Hikers can enjoy self-guiding trails or conducted day hikes. Roadside signs, exhibits, and viewpoints explain the park's natural features. Evening programs include films, slide programs, and talks. Information on park activities is available from bulletin boards or park information centers.

Visitors who wish to get away from the crowds may wish to investigate some of the conducted trips available. Several packers lead trips of varying lengths into the mountains. Hikers, rock climbers, and mountaineers will also find activities of special interest.

Types of camps

Canada's national parks all provide three kinds of campsites: serviced, semi-serviced, and primitive. A serviced campground has a full-time caretaker, and sometimes a matron in attendance, and facilities generally include electricity, plumbing, laundries, showers, and sewer connections for trailers.

A semi-serviced campground has part-time supervision, and provides kitchen shelters, stoves, fuel,

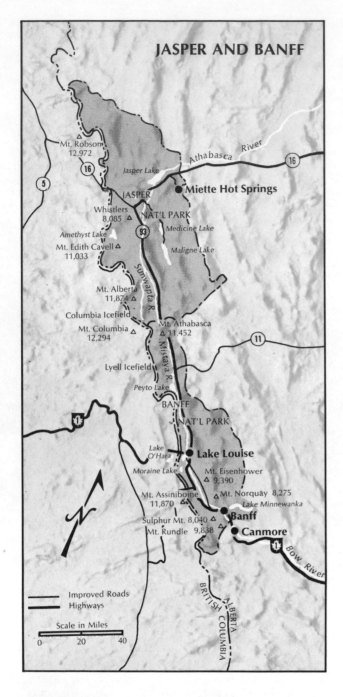

JASPER AND BANFF

Mt. Robson
12,972

Jasper Lake

Athabasca River

JASPER

Miette Hot Springs

Whistlers
8,085

NAT'L PARK

Medicine Lake

Amethyst Lake

Mt. Edith Cavell
11,033

Maligne Lake

Mt. Alberta
11,874

Sunwapta R.

Columbia Icefield

Mt. Columbia
12,294

Mt. Athabasca
11,452

Mistaya R.

Lyell Icefield

Peyto Lake

BANFF

NAT'L PARK

Lake O'Hara

Lake Louise

Moraine Lake

Mt. Eisenhower
9,390

Mt. Assiniboine
11,870

Mt. Norquay 8,275

Lake Minnewanka

Sulphur Mt. 8,040

Banff

Mt. Rundle 9,838

Canmore

Bow River

BRITISH COLUMBIA

ALBERTA

Improved Roads
Highways

Scale in Miles
0   20   40

water and toilets, while the primitive ones, usually inaccessible by car, may have only toilets, tables and fireplaces, sometimes a shelter, with water from a nearby stream.

Charges per night in the parks are $1.50 for an unserviced site, $2 for one with electricity, $2.50 for a site with piped water, electricity, and sewer connections. Camping, in most areas from late May to early October, is on a first-come, first-served basis, and usually limited to a stay of two weeks. Permission must be obtained from wardens for camping outside the regular sites. Dogs and other pets must be on leash at all times.

Other fees

The regulation $2 auto license, $1 for a trailer, entitles you to enter any Canadian national park as often as you like for the year beginning April 1. No hunting is allowed, and a special $2 fishing license is required to fish in the parks.

BANFF NATIONAL PARK

Banff became Canada's first national park in 1885. Canadian Pacific Railway workmen had found hot mineral springs gushing from the side of Sulphur Mountain, and by order of Queen Victoria's government, because the springs promised to be "of great sanitary advantages to the public," 10 square miles were set apart. Now the park encloses 2,564 square miles of spectacular scenery.

Getting there

The Canadian Pacific Railway arrives at Banff once from the east, and once from the west every day. Greyhound Bus Lines have five trips a day between Calgary and Banff in summer. There is weekend limousine service from the Calgary Airport, which is served daily by Air Canada, Canadian Pacific, Air West, and Western Airlines. Gray Line buses also connect Banff and Jasper.

Where to stay

Accommodations are largely in and around the community of Banff and at Lake Louise, 36 miles northwest. The venerable Banff Springs Hotel, with room for 1,080 guests, is now open the year around, and the equally famous Chateau Lake Louise has room for 708 guests. A great variety of cabin and motel accommodations is available.

In both Banff and Jasper Parks, rooms in private homes are available, often a great convenience to visitors who have not made advance reservations. Homes that rent rooms (inspected and approved by park officials) display signs in their windows.

Campgrounds are numerous. The largest ones, with complete facilities, are at Tunnel Mountain, Banff; at Two Jack Lake, 8 miles northeast of the townsite; at Johnston Canyon, 16 miles west; and at Lake Louise.

Seeing the park

Gray Line and Brewster Transport Company offer sightseeing tours out of Banff, some of which include cruises by launch on Lake Minnewanka, that go to Moraine Lake in the Valley of the Ten Peaks near Lake Louise, to Emerald Lake in Yoho National Park, to Radium Hot Springs in Kootenay, and, of course, to Jasper.

LOAFING on Mount Norquay, climber looks back on Banff townsite.

CASCADE MOUNTAIN looms above Banff Avenue, town's main street. Park accommodations are centered here and at Lake Louise.

Skyrides by gondola provide dramatic views. Four-passenger gondolas swing up Sulphur Mountain, 2½ miles from Banff, in an 8-minute ride, as the Bow River Valley and its surrounding mountains appear in ever-widening panorama. Banff is at a 4,550-foot elevation. The sky ride takes you from 5,194 feet to the 7,486-foot level, where a tea house serves "pie in the sky." All-day operation continues from May 1 through October. In winter, double chair lifts replace the gondolas.

On Mount Norquay, 5 miles northwest of town, 4-seater cablecars glide up a steep, 7-minute climb to the 7,000-foot level. Views from here are of the opposite side of the Bow Valley, with Mount Rundle reaching 9,838 feet above sea level. The cablecars operate all year. On top, the Cliffhouse serves meals and there are picnic tables on the high terrace.

The Whitehorn sedan lift, in 2 and 3-seat gondolas, makes a 20-minute, 2-mile run up the side of White-horn Mountain to look down on famed Lake Louise, a tiny gem in a setting of towering peaks. From mid-June through August, the lift operates from 9 A.M. to 6 P.M. There is a restaurant at the top.

By car, visitors using Banff as base should be sure to see these sights:

Vermilion Lakes, 3½ miles up river from town, three shallow lakes in the Bow Valley reflect the rocky heights of Mount Rundle and Sulphur Mountain (8,040 feet).

Lake Minnewanka, 8 miles northeast of town. On the way, circle through the paddock just off the highway on a mile-long loop to see the herd of plains buffalo there. Lake Minnewanka, 14 miles long, largest in the park, is walled by great cliffs that drop sheer to the water. Return on the road that passes Two Jack and Johnson Lakes.

The Hoodoos, glacial, eroded columns, seen from Tunnel Mountain Road. The road opens up to side views of the Sundance Range to the south, and Mount Norquay on the north.

By trail, any of a dozen lovely walks may be made in a day or less. One short hike (1.6 miles) goes to the top of Tunnel Mountain (5,500 feet) overlooking Banff and the Bow River Valley. Another, with no mountain climbing, follows the river downstream from the north end of Bow Bridge for one mile to Bow Falls, a good picnic spot, and continues across Tunnel Mountain meadows, bright with summer wildflowers, for a roundtrip of about 5 miles.

A 2½-mile hike starting on Spray Avenue passes

LOOKING ACROSS LAKE LOUISE, you see Victoria Glacier. This remnant of the Ice Age is still some 500 feet thick.

BAGPIPE echoes across Lake Louise as kilt-clad player marches.

the Banff Springs Hotel, and winds through pleasant woods to Upper Hot Springs, connecting there with a 3-mile trail up Sulphur Mountain. Frequently people ride up by gondola, and come down by the trail.

Maps outlining both motor and hiking routes are available at the park information center in the Museum Building on the north side of the Bow Bridge on Banff Avenue (open 8 A.M. to 9 P.M. in summer). Daily hikes are conducted by park naturalists. If you want to do any mountain climbing off the main trails, you must register and check out with a park warden in the Park Administration Building in Cascade Gardens, directly south of Bow Bridge.

By boat, pleasant cruising is available right in the Bow River at the edge of the townsite. The water is too swift for safety at the bridge, but a deep, smooth channel starting a little way above it extends upstream for 10 miles. Boats may be rented at the Bow River Boat House, about 1 block west of the south end of the bridge.

Echo Creek offers placid water for canoeing, and narrow Willow Creek, which joins Echo Creek and the first of the Vermilion Lakes, is ideal for canoeing. One-hour launch trips go up Bow River both morning and evening, starting in May.

Launch cruises of 1½ hours also sample Lake Minnewanka (5 trips a day in summer from 8 A.M. to noon). Boats, fishing tackle, and charter trips are available at Minnewanka.

By horseback, every July and August, Trail Riders of the Canadian Rockies explore the wilderness in the Banff and Lake Louise region. For nearly 50 years, this nonprofit organization, which has a Canadian president one year, an American the next, has been leading high country trail rides. Each summer there are four 6-day rides.

A day on the trail usually means a leisurely ride of about 15 miles, lunch beside a stream or lake, then back to base camp where tepees have been set up. In the evenings, the group gathers around the campfire for songs and stories.

For further information, write Trail Riders of the Canadian Rockies, P. O. Box 6742, Station D, Calgary, Alberta.

Other things to do

Golf courses are at Banff Springs Hotel and at Canmore, 11 miles east of Banff. Shopping is fun in Banff because of the variety of shops that carry Canadian crafts, Scotch woolens, and English china.

Swimming in Banff's hot springs is possible all year. The hot sulphur water outdoor pool at Upper Hot Springs is open 8 A.M. to 11:30 P.M. all summer, and in winter from 2 to 9 P.M. on weekdays, and 10 A.M. to 9 P.M. on weekends, when skiers luxuriate in the 100° water.

The Cave and Basin, one mile beyond the Bow Bridge,

where the first mineral springs were discovered, has an indoor pool of sulphur water (88°) and a fresh water pool (80°), open mid-May to September, 9 A.M. to 4:30 P.M., and until 9:30 P.M. during July and August.

Cascade Gardens Park, back of the Administration Building, has shady benches set among brilliant summer flowers, and nature trails. Evening film programs about the geology, and the plant and animal life of the park are given here during summer months.

The Banff Park Museum, open 2 to 5:15 P.M. and 6:30 to 9 P.M. daily in summer, has specimens of mountain goats and sheep, birds and reptiles in its natural history exhibits.

The Luxton Museum at the south end of the Bow Bridge has an exceptional Indian collection.

The Banff School of Fine Arts and Centre of Continuing Education occupies a charming campus on the western slopes of Tunnel Mountain. A branch of the University of Calgary, it draws many students from the United States among the 1,300 or more who attend its annual summer sessions.

Courses are offered in various aspects of theater, music, ballet, painting, modern languages, writing, handicrafts, and photography. Its Summer Festival brings renowned artists from all over the world to appear in recitals, opera, concerts, and theatricals. All major performances are given in the Eric L. Harvie Theatre on the campus.

Banff Indian Days, traditional celebration of the Stony Indians, bring colorful events to Banff for five days in July. Tribes from all over the province set up their tepees, and take part, in full regalia on elaborately caparisoned horses, in parades and in a rough all-Indian rodeo.

To Lake Louise

The Trans-Canada Highway goes northwest from Banff for 36 miles to Lake Louise, joined at the halfway point by the Banff-Windermere Highway (93) from Kootenay National Park. About 6 miles before you reach the junction, stop at the pullout beside the cairn honoring General Dwight D. Eisenhower, a grand viewpoint from which to see the mountain named after him. Mount Eisenhower's rugged bulk is topped with massive layers of Cambrian sedimentary rock, some of the most ancient deposits in the Rockies.

Lake Louise

Probably one of the most photographed spots in the world is blue-green Lake Louise which lies in a cup in the mountains some 5,000 feet above sea level, its protecting rim of peaks pushing close. Mount Victoria,

BANFF SCHOOL OF FINE ARTS is dwarfed by Mount Rundle. You take courses here in the summer.

LAKE O'HARA, one of the prettiest lakes in the Canadian Rockies, lies amidst craggy scenery away from crowds and can be reached from Highway 1. A chalet offers overnight lodging.

11,365 feet high, is the dominant peak, and Mount Aberdeen (10,850 feet), Mount Temple (11,636 feet), and Pope's Peak (10,376 feet) spread protecting walls about the lake.

Only 1½ miles long and ¾ mile wide, but nearly 300 feet deep, the lake is still fed by the great glacier that formed it. You look right into Victoria Glacier when you gaze across the lake from the tall windows of the lounge in the old Chateau Lake Louise. Like rambling Banff Springs Hotel, this dignified dowager of an earlier day is still charming and still impressive; the hotel is open from early June to early September. The area has numerous other lodge, chalet, and bungalow accommodations, many open year around.

Trails near Lake Louise

Like Banff, Lake Louise is full of tourists in mid-summer. To find the serenity and silence of the high mountain wilderness, you must penetrate farther into it. Some wonderful trails climb from here to other high lakes. Mirror Lake, at 6,700 feet, is the nearest, only 2 miles from the Lake Louise shore.

Another half mile from Mirror Lake takes you to Lake Agness at 7,000 feet, and goes on for a 7-mile hike to the Plain of Six Glaciers. The direct route to the Six Glaciers makes a more gradual ascent over a 4-mile trail that first follows the Lake Louise shore.

Other walks reach Paradise Valley, and for the rugged hiker, the 14-mile trail via Paradise over rocky, 8,550-foot-high Sentinel Pass to Moraine Lake (at 6,190 feet) is an exciting one.

Moraine Lake, in the Valley of the 10 Peaks, is also accessible by car, a 9-mile drive that branches off the Lake Louise road. Ten jagged peaks, most of them higher than 10,000 feet, rise from the edge of the lake, which is set in a dramatic hanging valley.

Lake O'Hara for many people is the choicest of all. Limited accommodations are available in a mountain chalet. You can walk or ride horseback to the lake from the O'Hara Gate, located across the border in Yoho National Park (near where Highways 1 and 1 Alternate meet), or go by bus either from the gate or from the Chateau Lake Louise. Inquire about this either at the Chateau or at the Lake Louise Information center, which is also located at the junction of Highways 1 and 1A, west of Lake Louise townsite (open 8 A.M. to 8 P.M. in summer). The trip is so popular that if you want to stay overnight at the chalet, it is often necessary to make reservations a year ahead.

THE ICEFIELD HIGHWAY

Starting one mile from Lake Louise townsite, the Icefield (or Banff-Jasper) Highway skims across the top of the Rockies for 142 miles. Towering peaks are

SNOWMOBILE has open top so passengers can see crevasses, ice-falls, and moraines on tour.

THE COLUMBIA ICEFIELD

The Columbia Icefield, remnant of the Ice Age, is the greatest accumulation of snow and ice in the Rocky Mountains. For some 15 miles, it straddles the Continental Divide, covering approximately 130 square miles.

Three great rivers begin in its melt waters. The Athabasca crosses Alberta to become part of the Mackenzie River System flowing to the Arctic Ocean. The North Saskatchewan flows across the prairies to Lake Winnipeg, headed for Hudson's Bay. And the Columbia River, which reaches the Pacific Ocean after 1,210 meandering miles, is fed by tributaries from the western slopes of the immense icefield.

The Athabasca Glacier comes within a mile of the Icefield Highway, the rocky debris of its slow passage testifying to its gradual shrinkage. Except for 1961 and 1962, when it did not recede at all, the glacier has shrunk at the rate of about 100 feet a year.

Only a few years ago, the great tongue of snow and ice did extend to the highway. Now a side road climbs one mile above the moraine to the snow-mobile station, where tours run all day over the mass of ice.

You are 7,150 feet above sea level when you step into one of the fleet of glass enclosed snow-mobiles for a 45-minute guided trip about 3 miles up the icefield.

ATHABASCA GLACIER, 6 miles long, comes close to Banff-Jasper Highway. Motorists get a fine view. Turnouts are frequent.

VACATIONERS stop for lunch at picnic site along Icefield Highway.

etched on an ever-nearing skyline. Slim, dense spruce darkens lower slopes, and timberline—craggy, bare rock—looks near. Over wide, easy grades, the pavement parallels roadside streams so full of glacial silt they are almost white. Sometimes the mountains are deep brown, sometimes topped with snow that spills over the sides and lies along horizontal ledges.

Picnic tables near the highway, chalets, youth hostels, and lakeside campgrounds beside spur roads are every few miles. Peak after peak reaches to 9,000 and 10,000-foot heights, and sometimes, like Mount Hector and Mount Athabasca, above 11,000 feet.

Viewpoint turnoffs are frequent; one of the loveliest is ¼ mile off the highway from the summit of Bow Pass, where you look straight down at glacial green Peyto Lake 600 feet below. A 1¼-mile trail goes down to it. The Banff-Jasper Parks boundary is at Sunwapta Summit (6,675 feet), about 74 miles north of the Lake Louise junction. About 3 miles further north, a side road goes right up into the Columbia icefields.

The highway is open from early May until the end of October, and during daylight hours in winter.

JASPER NATIONAL PARK

Second largest of Canada's national parks, Jasper's 4,200 square miles of high mountain wilderness were set aside as a national preserve in 1907. The park was named for a Missouri trader, Jasper Hawes, who was in charge of a North West Company trading post built at Brule Lake about 1813.

The park is open throughout the year, but many facilities operate only from May to September.

The charming, mountain-ringed community of Jasper is 31 miles from the park's eastern entrance on Highway 16, and 228 miles from Edmonton. It is served by Canadian National Railway, Greyhound Bus Lines, Coachways System, British Columbia Coachlines, and Brewster Transport.

Where to stay

Most accommodations are either in or within a few miles of the town of Jasper, although there are lodges off the Icefield Highway, and in the northeastern corner of the park, like Miette Hot Springs Motel, 38 miles northeast of the town, which can take care of 156 guests. Resorts with lodge and bungalows are numerous.

Luxurious Jasper Park Lodge, 4½ miles east of town on Lac Beauvert, with both lodge and cedar cabins, is one of Western Canada's most famous resorts, with accommodations for 763 guests.

Activities

Shopping is chiefly along Connaught Drive, the townsite's main street, where shops specialize in British

JASPER SKY TRAM gives you a magnificent view as it ascends at a rate of 600 feet per minute.

FROM INSIDE TRAM, you see a panorama of the Rockies, the town of Jasper, and the Athabasca River.

and Scandinavian imports—bone china, woolens, sweaters, Scotch tartans as well as Canadian handicrafts, paintings, and native gem jewelry.

Tours operated daily by Jasper Park Transportation coaches go to such places as the Glacier of the Angel on Mount Edith Cavell, Maligne Canyon (9 miles), Medicine Lake (18 miles), Miette Hot Springs, and Mount Robson on the other side of the Yellowhead Pass. All these destinations, of course, may be reached in your own car. Pick up maps for motor and walking trips at the park's information center beside the Canadian National Railway on Connaught Drive.

Maligne Lake was not accessible by auto until 1970. The power boat ride to the end of the lake is one of the park's scenic highlights. The far basin is surrounded by enormous rock faces hung with glaciers. The light green color of the water is the result of glacial silt.

A mile above sea level, Maligne, largest lake in the Rockies, is surrounded by snow-crested peaks of the Queen Elizabeth Range, most of them higher than 10,000 feet, while Mount Brazeau at the lake's far southern end, tops 11,000 feet. Closeup views of their massive glaciers open up after the launch noses through the Narrows, where camera fans like to photograph the tiny conifer-crowned spit of land that at high water is an island.

Seventeen miles long, the lake has a 50-mile shore-line, and fishermen find plentiful Eastern brook trout in its emerald waters.

Maligne Canyon and Medicine Lake

The drive to Maligne Lake is one of the most interesting ones out of Jasper because it passes Maligne Canyon and Medicine Lake on the way. The nearly straight up and down limestone walls of the canyon have been gouged out by centuries of stream erosion until in some places the canyon is almost 200 feet deep.

Medicine Lake, which "disappears" each winter, is 5 miles long, almost a mile wide, and 50 to 60 feet deep in summer. Come winter, all that is left is a shallow stream amid gravel bars. Great holes in the lake bottom drain it nearly dry then, but during warm months, snowmelt fills the lake faster than the water drains away.

Mountain climbing by air

The Jasper Sky Tram takes you sailing through the sky for a magnificent sky view of the Canadian Rockies. In 30-passenger cars, you whisk up Whistlers Mountain for 1¼ miles. You start at 4,226 feet and step out at the Upper Station at an elevation of 7,500 feet.

As the smooth-riding tram rises, Jasper townsite seems to grow tinier, the Athabasca and Miette

SPRING FISHING is excellent in park rivers. Here a fisherman tries his luck in the Maligne River.

Rivers turn into twisting ribbons, while tier on tier of snow-ridged peaks appear—the tip of that monarch of the Rockies, Mount Robson, showing on the western horizon. Cantilevered decks angle out over the mountainside from the tea house anchored to its rocky ledge.

Miles of trails lead across the slopes of Whistlers, named for the whistling marmots that live among its rocks. The Sky Tram Lower Station is 5 miles from Jasper.

Hiking and riding

Many trails, from short walks to 20-mile treks, are carefully marked for hikers and horseback riders. A map with some half-dozen routes outlined on the back is available at the information center in Jasper, and topographical maps of the park may be bought there as well.

Old Fort Point, where a North West Company trading post was built in 1811, is easily reached by a half-hour walk from the Jasper townsite. It climbs a rocky knoll above the east shore of the Athabasca River.

Fur trader-geographer David Thompson, with 10 men, pushed through these ice-bound mountains in the winter of 1810-11 to discover and cross Athabasca Pass to the Columbia River. For many years afterward, freight carriers used this route across the mountains to reach the fur-trading post at Boat Encampment on the Big Bend of the Columbia River. The trail to Fort Point passes a monument of field stones commemorating Thompson and his exploration of this area.

On Mount Edith Cavell, a more strenuous hike starting at the Chalet crosses a moraine and climbs through forests of spruce, fir, and pine to alpine meadows with summer wildflowers. You need at least a half-day for this one.

The park service also conducts walking trips around Maligne Canyon, on Mount Edith Cavell, and on Whistlers Mountain. And there are self-guiding nature trails like the pot-hole trail around Lake Annette (an easy 2 miles), the Sulphur Creek trail at Miette Hot Springs (1 mile), and the 1¼-mile Maligne Canyon trail. This one starts near the Maligne Canyon tea house, about 6 miles off Highway 16.

Certified guides are available for more advanced climbing, and both the Sierra Club and the Seattle Mountaineers have annual climbing camps in the Jasper high country.

The Sawdust Trail (12 miles), popular with riders, samples lodgepole country and deep spruce forest, and has great views of Mount Edith Cavell. (Mount Cavell, once called the Great White Mountain, was renamed for the British nurse, Edith Cavell, following World War I.)

Berg Lake, located in Mount Robson Provincial Park, British Columbia, can be reached by way of the Valley of the One Thousand Falls, and is an exciting ride.

Tonquin Valley is a favorite 2 to 3-day trip for riders, and hikers use the trails, too. The 5 to 6-hour riding pack trip provides almost every aspect of mountain scenery—meadows blue with lupine, white-riffled streams, delicately tinted Amethyst Lake (fishermen will find plenty of Eastern brook and native rainbow trout here), the sheer and rugged Ramparts, and at the end of a day's ride, heated tents or cabins for a comfortable night's rest.

One route starts from the viewpoint near Mount Edith Cavell, climbs a high trail, and ends at a camp near the chalet.

Another trail starts from the highway at Portal Creek, climbs to a point over 7,000 feet, and follows along Maccarib Creek, ending at the camps at the northern end of Amethyst Lake. A usual bonus on this trip is sighting caribou. Maccarib is an Indian word for caribou.

Several pack outfits lead trail rides into the back country. You can inquire at the information center to find out about these trips.

FOR FISHERMEN

The main rivers that drain glaciers in both Banff and Jasper National Parks are best for fishing in spring, before their waters are high and turbid with summer snow melt, and in the autumn. But the lakes number into the hundreds, and in them are lake, rainbow, cutthroat, brown, Eastern brook, and Dolly Varden trout, Rocky Mountain whitefish, and graylings.

On the following lakes, the season opens on Victoria Day, the last Monday in May, and closes September 30: in Banff Park, Lakes Minnewanka, Two Jack, Vermilion, Ghost, Johnson, Copper, and Kingfisher. In Jasper Park: Pyramid, Patricia, Annette, Medicine, Beaver, Maligne, Mona, Lorraine, and Jacques.

The season on many other lakes opens June 15 and closes October 15. Licenses may be purchased from park warden stations, park information centers, and administration offices. If you do not have your own gear along, rods and tackle may be rented at sport shops. And as any expert angler already knows, the best fishing is usually done in early morning and early evening.

HORSEBACK RIDERS pass the rugged Ramparts on the way to Tonquin Valley. Several packers lead two and three-day trips into this area. Heated tents or cabins await tired riders.

SKIERS relax for a few minutes at Marmot Basin, in Jasper National Park. Skiing lasts here until late May.

IT'S LATE MAY at Parker Ridge, Columbia Icefield. Not a cloud in the sky for perfect spring skiing.

SKIING THE ROCKIES

Banff and Jasper National Parks are the great winter playground of the Canadian Rockies. Four great ski areas noted for the dry powder of their broad slopes draw skiers from November into May. The skiable terrain is so extensive, the facilities so numerous, that despite crowds, there is seldom more than a few minutes wait for a lift.

Mount Norquay

Nearest to Banff, Mount Norquay is renowned for its 2-mile downhill course with a drop of some 2,000 feet, and its Olympic standard jump. The double chair lift whisks skiers up 1,350 vertical feet here. Daily operation, beginning November 15, is from 9 A.M. to 4 P.M., and to 5 P.M. toward the April 15 close of the season. A big bonus at Banff is to ski and then dive into the outdoor swimming pool of hot mineral water.

Lake Louise

Just off Highway 1, Lake Louise ski area is one of Canada's largest; average snowfall is 173 inches. Besides the 2-mile gondola climb up Whitehorn Mountain, Lake Louise has 2 double chair lifts, 4 pomas, and a T-Bar that run from late November to early May. Newest lift is the Olympic chair that rises 2,101 feet and is 7,000 feet long, with a capacity of 800 skiers an hour. Lifts from the upper terminal link two distinct regions for a 10-mile downhill circuit.

Greyhound buses bring skiers from Calgary to the depot at the Post Hotel, and Brewster Transport operates daily service from Banff. Buses also go from the Whitehorn car parking area to Mount Temple Chalet, which has 80 rooms for overnight accommodation. Numerous ski packages are available.

Sunshine Village

With a top elevation of 7,200 feet near the Continental Divide, Sunshine Village is 10 miles southwest of Banff on Highway 1, six miles to the Borgeau parking lot, then four miles by bus to the village. Skiing is from mid-November to mid-May.

Sunshine has 18 runs and 5 trails, 2 chair lifts, and 2 T-bars. Ski weeks are also available here. Daily operation is from 8:30 A.M. to 4 P.M. Overnight accommodations are available, and meals are served for day skiers at the lodge.

Marmot Basin

This ski area in Jasper National Park offers all types of skiing—from deep powder to packed snow slopes—from early November into late May. Thirteen runs

LONE SKIER cuts a trail across the untracked snow near the foot of Mount Assiniboine,
about 25 miles south of Banff. This area has not been developed; skiers go in by helicopter.

ASTOTIN LAKE in Elk Island National Park is popular for swimming, boating, water skiing.

SUMMER CRUISE BOATS on Waterton Lakes travel between Alberta and Glacier National Park.

range from gentle hills to the 7-mile run that starts at the mountain's 7,400-foot summit.

Eight miles southwest of Jasper townsite on Highway 93, the last 3 miles are by bus. Greyhound Buses serve the area from Edmonton, Banff, and Jasper, and Trailways Buses come north from Kamloops.

Marmot has no accommodations at the site, but two day chalets serve meals. A variety of ski weeks are offered every week except Christmas and Easter.

WATERTON LAKES NATIONAL PARK

Waterton Lakes National Park is 204 square miles of mountain scenery tucked into the far southwestern corner of Alberta. The park adjoins the United States' Glacier National Park in Montana. Together, lying astride the International Boundary, they form Waterton-Glacier International Peace Park, a first of its kind in the world.

The Canadian park was established in 1895, the American one in 1910. Rotary clubs of both Alberta and Montana promoted the idea of linking the two sanctuaries, and in 1932, the international park was created.

How to get there

Most American visitors come into Waterton Lakes from Glacier Park over Chief Mountain International Highway (6). Alberta's entrance is at the junction of Highways 5 and 6 on the park's eastern edge. Twice daily during summer, Greyhound buses make the 3-hour trip from Lethbridge to the park.

A snug park

Visitors often say they like the compactness of Waterton, the closeness of the mountains that slant down to highway, lake, and townsite, mountains noted for their vivid ocher and purplish coloration.

The lake is actually three lakes connected by straits that borrowed the names, Dardanelles and Bosporous, from the Aegean and the Black Seas. The sapphire waters of the mountain-walled waterway are half in the Canadian park, half in Glacier. The powerboat *International* cruises back and forth three times a day between Waterton and Goathaunt Landing in Montana.

Waterton is open all year, with limited facilities in winter, but the usual tourist season is from May to September. The town, which pushes out to the tree fringed edge of the lake, has a large heated, outdoor pool, a wading pool for children, horses to rent, free tennis courts, rental power and rowboats near the docks, and nearby an 18-hole golf course at the foot of 7,812-foot-high Mount Crandell.

There are more than a dozen motels and lodges in the town, with the grand old, many-gabled Prince of

Wales Hotel (open from June 15 to September 7) still providing its magnificent panorama of lake and mountain peaks. The largest campground is in Waterton itself, with 200 tent spaces and 95 trailer sites.

Highways and trails

Fifty miles of highways include popular drives like those to Cameron Lake and Red Rock Canyon. A 100-mile network of trails traverses alpine valleys, passes waterfalls, and leads to ice-edged tarns. Several of the high lakes have shelters for hikers.

ELK ISLAND NATIONAL PARK

An 8-foot wire fence surrounds Elk Island National Park—75 square miles of aspen parklands and shallow lakes—29 miles east of Edmonton via Highway 16. The park is dedicated to the preservation of the plains buffalo, and some 600 of the animals live here, along with elk, deer, and moose. Plains buffalo are displayed in a paddock near the southern entrance, and a small herd of pure wood buffalo range in a 24-square-mile area in the park's southwestern corner.

A north-south road bisects the park. Astotin Lake, 9 miles from the south gate, is popular for boating and water-skiing, with a campground on the eastern shore. The park has a 9-hole golf course, and an unusual exhibit—a thatch-roofed cottage similar to the ones Ukranian settlers built in the early 1900's.

Elk Island is open all year, but facilities are provided only from May through September.

WOOD BUFFALO NATIONAL PARK

This immense wild region in northeastern Alberta (and including part of Northwest Territories) is the largest game preserve in North America. Comprising 17,300 square miles, Wood Buffalo National Park lies between Lake Athabasca in Alberta and Great Slave Lake in the Northwest Territories. Running free here are some 12,000 bison, the largest remaining herd of bison on the continent. The park has no facilities for tourists in Alberta.

WILDLIFE IN THE NATIONAL PARKS

Visitors who hurry along the park highways in midsummer looking for wildlife are usually disappointed. But take off on a side road in early morning or late evening—feeding time—and watch along the edge of streams and lakes. You may have better luck.

Black bear inevitably show up at garbage dumps, sometimes even grizzlies at the more remote ones, although they prefer the back woods. If you do spot a grizzly, stay in your car—all wild animals are dangerous, but grizzlies are the most ferocious of all.

Look for moose in marshy valleys. They are frequently seen in the Vermilion Lakes area in Banff Park. Beavers are active here, too, but to see them requires much patience.

Mule deer and elk are common animals in the parks, though elk are more in evidence early and late in the season. Rocky Mountain bighorn sheep sometimes wander along main highways, and a good place to look for them is around Miette Hot Springs in Jasper Park. Only the male has the beautiful ¾ forward curve in his horns. The female's horns are short.

Rocky Mountain goats may frequently be seen on the highway as they visit the salt licks just east of Jasper townsite, and again along the highway 2 miles past Athabasca Falls. And turn your glasses on the south-facing slopes along the Icefield Highway. White as the snow on the mountain peaks, the goats have short, coal black horns.

GOATS *are often seen on or near the park highways. Sometimes they even stop traffic.*

SOUTHERN ALBERTA

Forts and frontier celebrations keep the days of the
Old West alive in prairie cities and towns

Travelers from Montana may cross the international boundary into Alberta by any of six entry points. Most people entering the province from British Columbia come across the Rocky Mountains either via the Trans-Canada Highway to Calgary, or, increasingly since the Yellowhead Route was opened, by Highway 16 to Edmonton.

ALONG HIGHWAY 3

One of the most comfortable roads, because it has the least traffic, is over Highway 3, which crosses British Columbia along its southern limits close to the United States border, and eases over the Continental Divide through Crowsnest Pass at an elevation of 4,453 feet. This is the same route used by the Canadian Pacific Railway for its southernmost tracks.

The Frank slide

The hamlet of Frank makes you aware of the massiveness of these mountains. For one mile, the highway runs through pale, broken boulders where an estimated 70 million tons of rock slid down Turtle Mountain in 1903, and in less than two minutes buried most of the residential section of what had been a booming coal town, killing some 70 persons.

The prairies

Swinging down out of the pass, the highway skirts coal and sawmill villages, and soon emerges onto high, rolling prairie. Now every community has the same silhouette: Rows of wooden grain storage towers beside the railway tracks, standing taller than the village church spires.

Southern loop

When you come into Alberta this way, you may want to turn south at Pincher Creek to visit Waterton Lakes National Park, 31 miles to the south. You can return through Cardston to Fort Macleod via Highways 5 and 2 to complete a 95-mile loop.

Cardston is known for its impressive Mormon Temple, constructed between 1913 and 1921, and the lovely gardens on the grounds. Charles Ora Card led Mormon pioneers from Utah to establish Canada's first Mormon settlement here in 1887. His house on Main Street is open to visitors daily in summer.

Lethbridge

Lethbridge, Alberta's third largest city (38,700 population), the center for a million acres of Southern Alberta's irrigated lands, is an attractive city of wide streets, spacious green parks, and climate tempered by warm chinook breezes out of the west. It has excellent hotel-motel accommodations.

Avenues run east and west in Lethbridge, streets north and south, and Highway 3 bisects the city. All streets north or south of it are so marked, with 14th Street the dividing line between east and west.

Lethbridge has both the University of Lethbridge and the two-year Lethbridge Community College, its

HENDERSON LAKE in Lethbridge is just the spot for an afternoon of fishing. You can rent paddleboats, and the park has a campground, picnic areas, playground, and Japanese garden.

own symphony orchestra, and enthusiastic theatrical groups. Developments are underway for an extensive new campus for the university on a scenic promontory above Oldman River.

The Genevieve E. Yates Memorial Centre, adjoining the City Hall, both contemporary structures on 10th Street off 4th Avenue South, has a small but pleasant art gallery (no admission charge), and a well designed little theater.

Henderson Lake Park, stretching along the east side of Mayor Magrath Drive, includes a golf course, shaded picnic areas and playgrounds, a campground, and a remarkable Japanese garden surrounding its pretty lake.

The campground at the eastern end of the lake, open from May 1 to October 1, has space for both tents and trailers.

The huge swimming pool is a wonderful place for family swims on hot summer days. Grassy banks for sunning and tree-shaded benches surround it. The pool is open daily from the first week in June through Labor Day, from 11 A.M. to 8 P.M.

There is an 18-hole golf course at the southern end of the park.

Man-made Henderson Lake is stocked annually with 100,000 rainbow trout. Youngsters fish from its

flat banks or from piers, while more experienced anglers generally use a boat. Boats, but no motors, may be rented at docks at the southern tip of the lake daily from 10 A.M. until dark.

Pathways meander over four acres in the Nikka Yuko Centennial Gardens in Henderson Lake Park, past pebble beaches, arched bridges, ponds, and gentle waterfalls. A wooden pavilion, first built in Japan, then dismantled and reassembled in Lethbridge, provides the proper setting for tea. Shoji walls slide open onto a dry garden.

Fort Whoop-Up

Like Fort Macleod, Lethbridge has its own fort, but this one, instead of honoring the work of the Mounties, recalls the very characters that the Mounted Police came west to subdue. A replica of the notorious Fort Whoop-Up stands in Indian Battle Park about 1 mile west of the center of town.

Originally, when the fort was built in 1869, it was known as Fort Hamilton. Once a scout was asked how things were going at Fort Hamilton, and he answered, "They are still whooping it up." After that it became Fort Whoop-Up.

Ox-drawn wagons used to creak up here from Fort Benton, Montana, bringing forbidden whiskey to

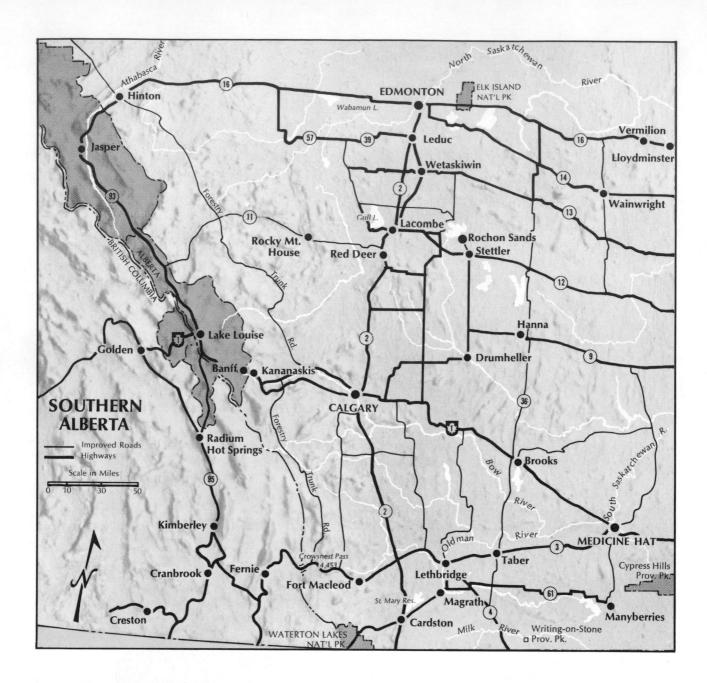

SOUTHERN
ALBERTA

— Improved Roads
━━ Highways

Scale in Miles
0 10   30   50

trade with the Indians for skins and buffalo robes. Now, within the fort's sharp-pointed log walls, are an old bull freight wagon and the 2-inch, muzzle-loading bronze cannon once used in the post.

Other displays have taped, push-button explanations. Most fun for youngsters is the tunnel ride on an old coal mine train. Outcroppings of coal were found in the gully here beside Oldman River, and by 1879 the North-West Coal and Navigation Company was sending coal to Medicine Hat by sternwheeler steamboat.

Indian Battle Park gets its name from the last great Indian versus Indian battle that took place here, when in 1870 the Blackfoot Indians defeated the Crees. The park has pleasant campsites and a playground.

Whoop-Up Days

The red and white striped flag with blue and white bands in the top left corner, which flies above Fort Whoop-Up, can be confusing on a breezy day. No Stars and Stripes, this, but the pennant the Montana traders raised whenever a new supply of whiskey was on hand. A close look reveals a double H formed by those blue bands. The letter stood for Healy and Hamilton (J. J. Healy and A. B. Hamilton) who operated the post.

Up and down the broad streets of Lethbridge, this flag is flown in early July when the annual Whoop-Up Days are in progress. The celebration, held in the Exhibition Grounds adjoining Henderson Park, continues for six days. Combining agricultural fair, stock judging, auctions, horse shows, rousing rodeos, and chuckwagon races, it all starts with a mammoth parade. Fair displays take in everything from pottery to pies, from cakes to cross-stitch.

Trips out of Lethbridge

Highways trail south from Lethbridge into Montana, and east to Saskatchewan. That province's capital, Regina, is 395 miles east via Highway 3.

St. Mary Dam, about 35 miles south by Highway 5, backs up the waters of the St. Mary River into an 11-mile-long reservoir that provides water for irrigating some 400,000 acres of southern Alberta.

Writing-on-Stone Provincial Park, which comprises more than 1,000 acres, is south of Lethbridge, 52 miles by Highway 4 to Milk River, then east on 26 miles of well graded road. This is a pretty drive through wheat farming country, with the Sweetgrass Hills of Montana on the southern horizon. For anyone interested in history as told by pictograph, this is one of the outstanding examples of this ancient art.

Most of the writings, incised into the rock, are on the northern walls of a coulee, at whose base is a pleasant cottonwood-shaded campground. The pictographs appear at various sites for approximately 1½ miles to the west.

Archaeologists consider that the most primitive depictions of animals and men here are very old indeed. Other drawings show historical changes in the natives' way of life. Some incisings show men with bows that were tipped on one end with spears. Horses appear in others, while still others portray men using guns. Thus the history of the local Indians is traced from the era of bows and spears through times that brought horses north from Mexico, and subsequently the white man's firearms from the east. Unfortunately some of the drawings have been defaced, but many are clearly distinguishable.

To the Saskatchewan border

Medicine Hat, thriving industrial city of approximately 25,500 population, is 105 miles east of Lethbridge by Highway 3. The drive is through farming lands in which wheat and sugar beets are prime crops.

All this southeastern corner of Alberta is a splendid upland bird hunting region, particularly for pheasants, ducks, Canada geese, and several varieties of grouse.

China Lakes, 14 miles south of Taber, a 30-mile-long waterway, makes a pleasant detour for swimming, boating, and fishing for Eastern brook, rainbow, brown, and cutthroat trout. At Medicine Hat, Highway 3 meets Trans-Canada Highway 1, which, 35 miles to the east, leaves Alberta on its long way across Canada.

FORT MACLEOD

The replica of Fort Macleod in the town still so called is one of Western Canada's best. Typical of the early western post, its 10-foot walls of sturdy logs are overhung at each corner with a square blockhouse sliced here and there with oblong slits just wide enough for the barrel of a rifle. The Canadian West's first Northwest Mounted Police fort, built in 1874, and named for its commander, Colonel James Macleod, it stood originally on an island in Oldman River.

The scarlet-coated Mounties had come 1,000 miles across the prairies on their thoroughbred horses to stop the illicit whiskey traffic which American traders were carrying on with the Indians. With living quarters inside the sturdy walls, the fort actually represented a small center of civilization in the vast prairie lands of the West.

Colorful Indian tepees, covered wagons, and cannons are within its walls now, and the museum displays wax figures of Mounties and Indians, a great stuffed buffalo, and a large variety of relics, from buffalo horn spoons to black angora goat-fur cowboy chaps.

One cottage built against the enclosing logs was the medical-dental center. Perhaps the whole fort presents a somewhat stylized version of western life in the 1800's, but the old dental chair, and the ruthless appearing equipment beside it, point up the less glamorous aspect of those rugged but romanticized days.

Hours are 8 A.M. to 9 P.M. daily.

FORT MACLEOD is an excellent replica of 19th-century North-West Mounted Police outpost.

CYPRESS HILLS PARK

The high hills of Cypress Hills Provincial Park rise abruptly from the prairie plateau 41 miles southeast of Medicine Hat to straddle the Alberta-Saskatchewan border. To get to the area, drive 20 miles east of Medicine Hat on Trans-Canada Highway 1, then turn south and drive 21 miles on Highway 48 to the park.

This fascinating area is in complete contrast to the surrounding plains. In this strange region of spruce, pine, and poplar, have been found fossils of prehistoric creatures—sabertooth cats, three-toed horses, and camels—that lived 30 million years ago in the Oligocene epoch.

Today the woods and grasslands of this park still provide refuge for dozens of varieties of wild animals, from squirrels and weasels to deer and wapiti.

The Cypress Hills have known the white man since the late 18th century. Captain William Clark of the Lewis and Clark Expedition passed through in 1806. Soon came traders, trappers, bootleggers —and trouble. Whiskey trade with the Indians was responsible for much of it. The region's increased lawlessness finally resulted in the formation of the North West Mounted Police in 1873. Even Sitting Bull and his band of Sioux retreated here for several years after the Battle of Little Big Horn in Montana.

Geographically, these hills form a major watershed divide; at their highest point, elevation is about the same as the town of Banff, nearly 200 miles to the west. Creeks to the south of the hills go into Milk River and the Missouri-Mississippi River system, while streams rising on the north head for Hudson's Bay via the waters of the Saskatchewan.

Because of the elevation of the hills, their luxuriant plant life, and cool streams, explorer Captain Palliser aptly called the area "an oasis in the desert." Much of the plant and insect life are common to the sub-tropics, possibly because this area was not glaciated during the last Ice Age, and thereby provided a haven for these small life species.

Alberta's largest provincial park, Cypress Hills has three campgrounds at Elkwater Lake, Reesor Lake, and Spruce Coulee.

Fishing is good for both northern pike and yellow perch at Elkwater Lake, for rainbow trout in Reesor Lake, and for eastern brook at Spruce Coulee. Boat rentals are available.

Many people who live on the surrounding plains go to the park simply for a refreshing day of swimming and water-skiing.

The park is open all year, and in winter it has skiing facilities.

Medicine Hat

Legend has it that during a battle between Cree and Blackfoot Indians, the Crees' medicine man deserted, losing his hat in the river. Others say that the town in the valley of the South Saskatchewan is shaped like an inverted hat. Regardless of derivation, the town with the colorful name today has half a dozen attractive parks, tree-lined residential streets, two golf courses, and a big Exhibition Grounds where Medicine Hat's own lusty stampede is held annually for three days in late July. Winding through town is the South Saskatchewan River, the name stemming from the Indian word *Kis-is-ska-tche-wan,* meaning "fast flowing water."

The community dates from the coming of the Canadian Pacific Railway in 1883. In that same year, the "Mounties" established a post where the Medicine Hat Golf and Country Club is now. It was also in 1883 that railway workers drilling a well for water struck gas. Now the city owns a reserve of gas estimated at some 730 billion cubic feet. One of the industrial plants open to visitors is Altaglass, where glass is manufactured both by the sculpture process, and by the old world method of blowing the molten material.

To Calgary

The quickest way from Lethbridge to Calgary (136 miles) is over Highway 2 up through the foothill country straight north from Fort Macleod. The last 50 miles of it is divided highway. Several provincial campgrounds are conveniently close to the road.

CALGARY

Calgary, with a population of 375,111 persons, reaches out over low, rolling foothills for an amazing 155 square miles. So famous is its annual Stampede that tourists seem to expect the city to have a western cowboy atmosphere all the time. Instead, they find a modern metropolis of towering office buildings and handsome homes, and 515 public parks, many of them along the banks of the two rivers that wind through the city—the Bow, and its tributary, the Elbow River, both of which start in the Canadian Rockies.

Calgary's very beginnings were at the point where the Elbow joins the Bow River, for the North West Mounted Police built a post there in 1875. The Hudson's Bay Company soon added a trading post, and in 1883 the railroad arrived, as Canadian Pacific Railway pushed its tracks across Canada.

Texas cowboys drove their cattle north into Canada's fine grazing lands, beginning a ranching industry which now brings more than $125 million worth of livestock through the Calgary stockyards every year. Grain also continues as a vital factor in Calgary's

WOODEN GRAIN STORAGE TOWERS line the railway tracks in Alberta prairie towns. Many of the growers belong to local cooperatives. These are in Nanton, south of Edmonton.

economy, but like Edmonton, oil and natural gas are the catalysts that made it the prosperous and fast growing city it is. Almost 400 Calgary-based firms are connected with the oil and gas industry, and the city is headquarters for more than half the petroleum companies in Canada.

Calgary's early days

The city became Calgary in 1876 when Colonel James Macleod named the post at Bow River after his home in Scotland, a small estate on the Isle of Mull. The name was said to mean "clear running water."

It was incorporated as "town of Calgary" in 1884, a year after the first train had arrived from Winnipeg. Oil was discovered in the Calgary district in 1913, but the industry received its first great boost in the following year when the Dingman Discovery well was activated in the Turner Valley. Thirty-eight wells came into production in the valley that year.

Information centers

Visitors can find two Hospitality Houses, one in the center of the city beside Husky Tower, the other at

Mewata Park beside "5934," the last of the massive steam locomotives used to pull trains over the Rockies before the more efficient diesels forced them into retirement. Maps, brochures, accommodation guides, and complete information on what to see and do in the area are available at each of the two centers the year around. In summer, a Hospitality House is also open at each major entrance to the city.

Where to stay

Most of the big hotels are in the downtown area, which extends approximately between 4th and 9th Avenues, and between 10th Street West and 4th Street East. Extensive motel strips line the main highways through town—Highway 2, which bisects the city north and south, and Highway 1 east and west.

The Alberta Tourist Guide lists nearly 70 approved hotels and motels. But even with this accommodation complex, it is necessary to make reservations well in advance for rooms during the Calgary Stampede in July, because such huge crowds attend the event. If you have difficulty in finding accommodations, the Calgary Tourist and Convention Association, Mewata Park, is glad to help.

CALGARY'S HUSKY TOWER dominates the city's skyline. It has a 200-seat, revolving restaurant from which you can look across the prairie to the snow-capped peaks of the Rockies.

Getting around

Calgary's streets run north and south, and its avenues go east and west. Northeast and northwest numbers are north of the Bow River, while southeast and southwest are south of the Bow, with Centre Street the dividing line.

Shopping and dining

The big department stores, including well known Canadian chains like Hudson's Bay and Eaton's, are found in the downtown district, along with many specialty shops and boutiques. Store hours are from 9 A.M. to 5:30 P.M., with most establishments remaining open until 9 P.M. on Thursdays and Fridays. Four major suburban shopping centers also feature large department stores.

Although Calgary restaurants cater to many tastes, Alberta beef is the featured, city-wide specialty. A lively city, Calgary has many night clubs.

Climate

High in the rolling prairies at an elevation of 3,438 feet, gateway to both summer and winter mountain sports, Calgary is only 81 miles from Banff. Warm in summer, cold in winter, but with low humidity, Calgary has a yearly average of 17½ inches of precipita-

tion, of which 5.85 is snow, while it averages more than 6 hours of sunshine a day the year around—an annual total of more than 2,200 hours.

Calgary's colleges

The University of Calgary officially opened its doors on its 300-acre campus in the city's northwest section in 1960. New buildings, new programs and degrees continue to be added. Full time registration is now about 7,000 students; but part-time, evening, and summer classes boost the total number of students to more than 10,000.

The Southern Alberta Institute of Technology, 1301 16th Ave. N. W., also has an enrollment of some 6,000 in day courses, and 5,000 in evening classes.

The Mount Royal Junior College, 7th Avenue and 11th Street S. W., founded in 1910, became affiliated with the University of Calgary in 1966.

City orchestras

Calgary has its own symphony orchestra of 70 musicians, which gives concerts each October to April season at the Southern Alberta Jubilee Auditorium. The Calgary Philharmonic Society also sponsors a Junior Philharmonic Orchestra, likewise made up of approximately 70 young musicians.

Places to see

There is a great deal to see and do in Calgary any time of year.

Husky Tower, 626 feet high, at 9th Avenue and Centre Street, provides a good viewpoint to get your bearings. It has an observation deck, cocktail bar, old English tavern, and revolving restaurant. From this high point, you look out across rolling rangelands that stretch in every direction beyond the city, the western horizon notched with the white peaks of the Rocky Mountains. The panorama at night above the city's myriad twinkling lights is magnificent.

Heritage Park is a good place to visit soon after your arrival in Calgary to get a glimpse of how the typical little "cow town" of the 19th century appeared. Proud of its tremendous growth from Mounted Police Post to flourishing, cosmopolitan city, Calgary has preserved its past in this complete pioneer village.

On 60 acres beside the Glenmore Reservoir in the Elbow River, at 82nd Avenue S. W. and 14th Street S. W., you see actual buildings of the pioneer era, a blacksmith shop where horses are being shod, a general store where you can buy cheese and gum drops and candy sticks, old-fashioned post office, quaint old barber shop with its bathtub behind a discreet curtain, and a real harness shop. And you may dine in hearty family style at the gracefully balconied old Wainwright Hotel, built in 1906.

You walk on plank sidewalks, ride a steam train, or cruise the lake on the *S. S. Moyie,* her big paddle wheel splashing away at the stern. The sternwheeler, which carries 172 passengers, is a half-size replica of Canadian Pacific Railway's *Moyie* that operated for the decade between 1880 and 1890 on the Kootenay Lakes of British Columbia.

The Jubilee Auditorium, Southern Alberta's identical twin to Northern Alberta's auditorium in Edmonton, was built by the provincial government in 1955 to mark Alberta's 50th anniversary.

Designed for performance of opera, symphony concert, theatrical presentation, exhibition, and large social gathering, each structure has a theater which will seat 2,750 persons. Satin walnut panelling that slopes inward at the top, and ceilings of plaster baffles achieve remarkably fine acoustics. The huge stage may be enlarged by raising the hydraulically operated floor of the orchestra pit.

Each building has spacious, beautifully lighted display galleries for paintings, sculpture, craft or other exhibits, and three social rooms which may be opened into one large room to seat 800 persons.

Free daily tours, except when special events are held, are conducted from noon to 5 P.M.

The Centennial Planetarium was built as a part of Canada's centennial observance in 1967. It uses five

HOCKEY GAME in one of Calgary's many community parks, green in summer and flooded in winter.

STERNWHEELER S. S. Moyie makes daily cruises on Glenmore Reservoir from Heritage Park.

CHUCKWAGON RACES are exciting events at the Stampede. Each driver has four outriders, who encourage but can't help driver.

INDIANS at Stampede, like Chief Walking Buffalo, wear full regalia.

telescopes, and up to 250 people can sit in its theater to watch space-age sky shows. This contemporary complex, of intriguing architectural design, also has a lecture theater and a science museum. Open daily except Tuesday, shows are given both afternoons and evenings.

The Calgary Zoo on St. George's Island in the Bow River, right in the center of town, has much to offer. On the long island are both a prehistoric display of life size dinosaurs, and a great 20th century collection of wildlife.

The first exhibits 46 different full-scale replicas of the enormous creatures that roamed Alberta 100 to 200 million years ago.

The adjoining zoo contains some 1,300 live animals from all over the world. Youngsters can play with live pets in the miniature zoo. Hours are 8 A.M. to dusk daily; in summer there is an admission charge.

The Calgary Aquarium, at 9th Avenue and 15th Street S. E., offers a glimpse of sea life—giant turtles from the South Seas, sturgeon, strange albino trout, and other marine life, all in well lighted tanks. Salt water is trucked from the Pacific Ocean for the sea exhibits. There is also a trout hatchery here.

Horseman's Hall of Fame is located on the second floor of the aquarium building. This unusual exhibit features ranch and rodeo horses, and the famous horsemen who rode them.

The Glenbow Museum, operated by the Glenbow Foundation and the provincial government, in the old Courthouse at 530 7th Ave. S. W., has a varied assortment of memorabilia. It includes some natural history, mineral displays, porcelains and ceramics, artifacts that depict the customs of the Indians of Canada's western plains, with special emphasis on the dress and doings of the pioneers.

Hours are 10 A.M. to 9 P.M. Tuesday through Friday, 10 A.M. to 5 P.M. Saturday, 11:30 A.M. to 6 P.M. Sunday, and 10 A.M. to 5 P.M. Monday.

Happy Valley, 5 miles west of Calgary, just off Highway 1, caters to family recreation—both indoor and outdoor—with swimming, golf on a miniature links or a pitch and putt course, horseback riding over bridle trails through the valley's 200 acres, fishing, picnicking, and, in winter, skating and tobogganing.

The Calgary Stampede

During 10 days early in July every year, Calgary turns into one of the West's most flamboyantly colorful, exciting, frontier-flavored cities, when its famed Stam-

THE CALGARY STAMPEDE draws the experts—the champion cowboys and the toughest broncs. "Stampede fever" takes over the town each year during the 10-day celebration in July.

pede takes place. Back in 1912, the first one was held as a nostalgic farewell to the erstwhile pioneer cattle era. Hardly a farewell now, it is more a welcome return to the wild, free days of that early West.

"Stampede fever," they call it, as Calgarians and visitors alike take to the traffic-free streets in their white cowboy hats and high-heeled boots, and their full-skirted flounces, to square dance from 9 o'clock in the morning to noon day after gala day. These are days that begin with flapjack breakfasts served from chuckwagon tailgates while Indians, Mounties, and pioneers in antique coaches tour the downtown area.

Out at the livestock pavilion, prize cattle, horses, sheep, and swine are on display. Here, 4-H Club youngsters stage their annual show and sale. As many as 30,000 people fill the grandstand daily to watch 10 days of championship performances—cowboys testing their strength atop Brahma bulls, roping calves, riding wild steers, leaping from a horse to "bulldog" the horns of a steer and wrestle the animal to the ground, sometimes in less than five seconds.

Barrel racing and wild cow milking are part of the shows that every evening are climaxed with the free-for-all chuckwagon races. Four wagons at a time, each with a team of four horses, and each with its four outriders, careen around the long oval in a rousing clatter of pounding hooves, creaking wagons, and

shouting cowboys, all in a wild swirl of dust.

After that come the grandstand music and dance extravaganzas, and finally, the late evening fireworks. During the 10 days, Indians of the Blackfoot, Stony, Sarcee, and Peigan tribes live on the Exhibition Grounds in brightly decorated tepees. In their buckskin and beads, and their feathered headgear, they join red-coated Mounties, bands, drum corps, and elaborate floats in long parades. And every night all over town, every cabaret and night club puts on its own version of western entertainment.

So popular is the Stampede that visitors are advised to send for seats well ahead by writing to Calgary Exhibition and Stampede, Limited, Box 1060, Calgary 2, Alberta.

OUT OF CALGARY

Trans-Canada Highway 1 veers southeast of Calgary for 182 miles to Medicine Hat. About 30 miles northeast of Brooks in Dinosaur Provincial Park, on the Red Deer River, you can camp where dinosaurs once roamed.

The Badlands

These are Alberta's Badlands, 200 miles of strangely eroded rock scoured out by the Red Deer River, an

WORN CHIMNEYS are all that remain of original Fort Rocky Mountain House, early fur-trading post.

RED DEER CITY PARK in front of City Hall is for walkers only—not even a bicycle is allowed.

area known to paleontologists all over the world, but little known to travelers. The park takes in some 22,000 acres, a queer bronze-shaded land of grotesque shapes, where scientists have unearthed prehistoric treasures—dinosaur skeletons, crocodile and oyster shell fossils, and the clear imprint in rock of such plants as yucca, ginkgo, and palm trees, from the time when this was a semi-tropical inland sea.

You do not have to drive this far for a look at the Badlands, however. Drumheller, 86 miles northeast of Calgary on Highway 9, lies in the Red Deer Valley, once Canada's greatest source of coal. It is the take-off point for the "Dinosaur Trail," a 30-mile drive that passes weird "hoodoos," or strange rock shapes, and prehistoric graveyards where whole skeletons of dinosaurs have been found.

Before you take the drive, see the exhibits in the Drumheller and District Museum on First Street East, which also houses the information center.

The Valley has been the most prolific hunting ground for dinosaurs in the world, as erosion has crumbled the soft rock, exposing their bones. Last of these enormous creatures to live in swampy edges of the inland sea existed here some 70 to 75 million years ago. The first dinosaur skull was discovered in the valley in 1884. Much about the way these creatures lived, how their remains were preserved in the river banks, and the work done here by paleontologists is explained in the museum.

West to Banff

The ski slopes of Banff National Park are an easy 81 miles west of Calgary over the Trans-Canada route, divided highway nearly all the way. Outside the park in the Kananaskis Valley, 71 miles from Calgary, Snowridge, at a base elevation of 6,000 feet, (7,600 feet at the top level) also has great skiing, as well as tobogganing, skating, and skidooing.

North to Edmonton

To the north, the old Calgary and Edmonton Trail, once an Indian path, then a wagon road, is now divided highway for most of its 186 miles. In 1883, the Royal Mail was being carried between the two communities by wagon, and the first stagecoach was jouncing passengers over the road, a 5-day excursion.

Red Deer

This pretty town, through which flows the Red Deer River, has nearly 27,000 residents. Like so many of Alberta's cities, it has wide, clean streets, and acres of parks, one of which, the City Hall Park, is right in the center of town. It offers good hotel-motel accommodations, and an inviting wooded campground on the riverbank.

Both east and west of Highway 2 in this region of

rolling prairies called the Parklands, provincial parks are situated beside the sandy shores of lakes that yield pike and perch. Streams that race down out of the snowfields of the Rockies give up rainbow and cutthroat trout, goldeyes, and sometimes Arctic graylings. And the fishing does not stop in winter; on a sunny Sunday afternoon, several hundred anglers may drop their lines through the ice of Pine Lake, 26 miles southeast of Red Deer, and take home good catches of perch.

The David Thompson Highway

From Rocky Mountain House, 48 miles west of Red Deer, Highway 11, called the David Thompson Highway, follows the North Saskatchewan River to Banff National Park. The river was the route of the earliest fur traders, and a post was established by the North West Company at Rocky Mountain House in 1799. Explorer David Thompson set out from here in 1807 on his trek to the mouth of the Columbia River.

Winter time

Many Alberta towns greet the winter season with special celebrations like Wetaskiwin's annual carnival during the third week in February. Every community of any size has both skating and curling rink, and many towns, like Red Deer, Camrose, Wetaskiwin, Wainwright, and others, have nearby ski hills. At Red Deer's Canyon Ski area, for example, a snow machine adds continually to nature's own supply of white stuff.

ADVENTURE HIGHWAY

The Forestry Trunk Road, built originally as a fire road, is used more and more by travelers who want a taste of wilderness. It is Western Alberta's wilderness route, starting from Beaver Mines south of Pincher Creek, and wriggling over 400 miles northward along the Rocky Mountain foothills all the way to Highway 2 at Goodwin, 26 miles east of Grand Prairie. Campers and hunters must register at the nearest ranger station both when entering and leaving the road.

Although this is roughing-it country, the road is seldom very far from access roads, either into the well traveled national parks or east to populated central Alberta. Red Deer River Crossing, 59 miles northwest of Cochrane, has one small mountain lodge, and the only service station on the road.

The road is sprinkled with campgrounds, however (see Sunset's *Western Campsite Directory*). Most have a few tent and small trailer spaces (no oversize trailers are allowed on the road), but many are only picnic stops, with several tables and fireplaces, and perhaps a shelter. Drinking water is usually from nearby creeks. Views of snow crested mountains, silent alpine meadows bright with summer wildflowers, and clear streams in their first rush down wooded hillsides can compensate for a lot of accustomed comforts.

Fishing is wonderful in the streams. Try the Oldman and the Livingstone Rivers north of Pincher Creek, and the Ram River south of Nordegg for cutthroat trout. The Oldman and the Bow systems have rainbow trout; the Highwood and the Red Deer, Rocky Mountain whitefish. Smaller rainbow and brook trout, Dolly Vardens, and whitefish are found in dozens of brushy creeks.

This is also big game country, home to moose, bighorn sheep, Rocky Mountain goat, elk, mule and whitetail deer, and black and grizzly bear.

RIVERS AND STREAMS are within easy reach of the Forestry Trunk Road which winds leisurely along the foothills. Picnic areas and campsites are scattered along the road.

NORTHERN ALBERTA

Dinosaurs once roamed this vast region. You follow the
trails of the Indians, trappers, and gold seekers

Alberta's cities come as surprises, springing up out of
the prairie with their broad, clean streets, shady parks,
and rambling streams. But Edmonton, Alberta's capital and Canada's fourth largest city, is the biggest
surprise of all.

EDMONTON

The elegant contemporary buildings of this city rise
higher and higher on green hills above a curling river,
the North Saskatchewan. The stream bisects the city,
and its whole green, wide valley—35 miles of river
banks—has been dedicated to public use, picnic
grounds, shady trails, fish ponds, and golf courses.
Indeed, Edmonton is said to have more parks per
capita than any other city in Canada.

Along the winding river, arched over with eight
bridges, these stretches of lawn and trees offer one
charming view after another. Natural gas in seem-
ingly unlimited abundance is the predominant fuel
used throughout the city; this is one of the reasons
that Edmonton claims such clear skies. It also boasts
one of the lowest pollen counts in the world.

Climate

Edmonton is hot in summer, with temperatures during July and August ranging from the 70's into the
low 90's. It is also cold in winter, with an average
temperature of 10°, which dips to the minus 40's for
brief periods. Edmontonians, however, invariably
insist, "But you don't feel it because it is so dry."

On summer evenings, daylight lasts until 10 o'clock,
and on autumn nights, the aurora borealis often lights
the sky with its streaming colors. Surveys have found
the year-around daily average of sunshine is over 6
hours; in midsummer months the city has up to 17
hours a day of clear sunshine.

Tourist information

Edmonton has four visitor bureaus. Driving up Highway 2 from the south, you'll find one at 5068 103rd
St., open daily all year from 9 A.M. to 5 P.M., and
until 9 P.M. in summer (May 15 to September 15).

The downtown bureau, 10145 100th St., is open
all year on weekdays from 9 A.M. to 5 P.M., and every
day until 9 P.M. during the mid-May to mid-September season.

The other two offices, one on Highway 16 West (on
the road to Jasper National Park), and the East End
Bureau, 3812 118th Ave., both maintain 9 A.M. to
9 P.M. hours 7 days a week during summer.

Escort service

Not only do these information centers provide maps,
brochures, and the Alberta Tourist Guide, which lists
all government-approved accommodations throughout the province, along with tent and trailer camps,
but they offer a unique scooter escort service for
visitors.

During July and August, the "Klondike Kids," 16

MIDTOWN EDMONTON is burgeoning with high-rise apartments and offices. Alberta's capital and Canada's fourth largest city, Edmonton rises abruptly from the surrounding prairie.

to 18-year-olds, precision trained for this special duty, stand by at each visitor bureau to lead travelers anywhere in the city without charge.

The city speed limit is 30 miles an hour, and, as throughout Western Canada, drivers generally obey the rules far better than drivers do in the States.

Transportation

Air Canada, Canadian Pacific Airlines, and Pacific Western Airlines all serve Edmonton, as well as Canadian National, Canadian Pacific, and Northern Alberta Railways, Greyhound Line of Canada, and Coachways System.

The usual car rentals are available, listed in the telephone directory, and the local Edmonton Transit System offers convenient bus service all over the city. You can find out where to catch what bus by calling 439-4971.

Tours

The Gray Line offers a variety of coach trips around Edmonton, and you can also do your own exploring by car with the aid of an official city map available at any of the four visitors' bureaus.

Two tours are outlined on the back of the map, each timed for about an hour and a quarter. One includes the western side of the city, the other takes in the eastern perimeter and the industrial section. The routes also are marked along the streets by "City Tour" signs, one red, the other blue.

How to get around

Avenues run east and west in Edmonton, with the avenue numbers climbing as you go north, while streets run north and south, their numbers increasing as you go west.

Downtown is approximately between 100th and 104th Avenues, and 100th and 104th Streets; this includes the handsome Civic Centre, and the main department stores and shops. Most stores stay open until 6 P.M. and to 9 P.M. on Thursdays and Fridays.

Accommodations

Alberta's Tourist Guide lists more than 60 approved hotels and motels in Edmonton. Nevertheless, rooms should be reserved a good six weeks ahead for Edmonton's Klondike Days celebration in July.

Most of the big hotels, like Canadian National

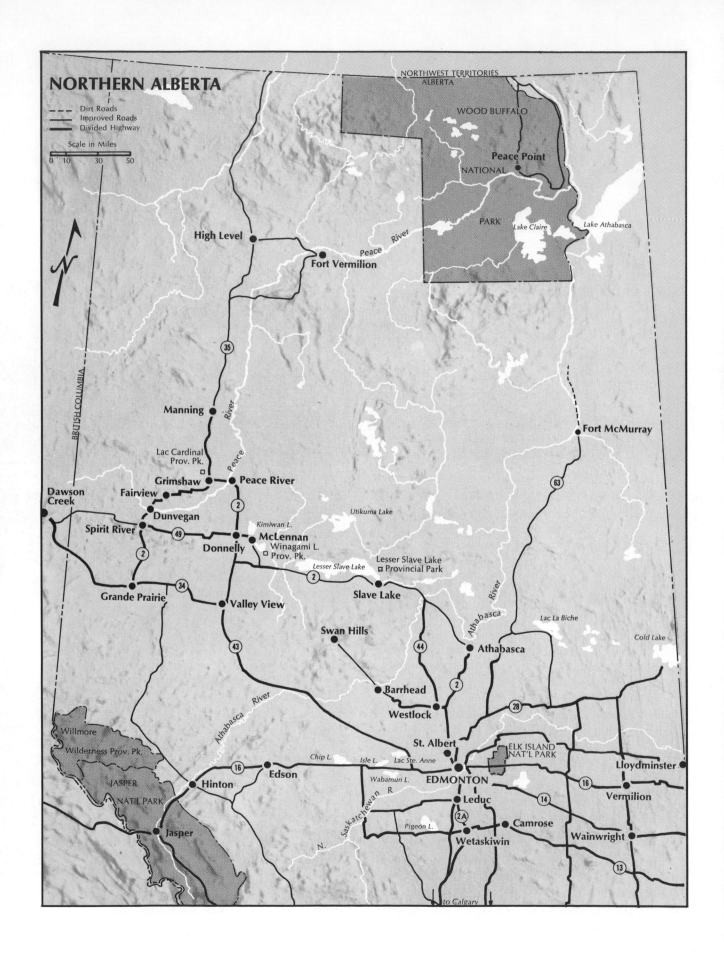

NORTHERN ALBERTA

Dirt Roads
Improved Roads
Divided Highway

Scale in Miles
0 10   30   50

NORTHWEST TERRITORIES
ALBERTA

WOOD BUFFALO

Peace Point

NATIONAL

PARK

Lake Claire

Lake Athabasca

Peace River

High Level

Fort Vermilion

BRITISH COLUMBIA

(35)

Manning

Fort McMurray

Lac Cardinal
Prov. Pk.

Grimshaw   Peace River

Fairview

Dunvegan   (2)

Dawson
Creek

Utikuma Lake

(63)

Spirit River   (49)   Kimiwan L.

McLennan

Donnelly   Winagami L.
Prov. Pk.

Lesser Slave Lake

Lesser Slave Lake
☐ Provincial Park

(2)

(2)

Grande Prairie   (34)

Valley View   Slave Lake

Athabasca River

Lac La Biche

Cold Lake

Swan Hills

(43)

(44)

Athabasca

Barrhead   (2)

Westlock   (28)

Willmore

Wilderness Prov. Pk.

St. Albert

ELK ISLAND
NAT'L PARK

JASPER

Chip L.   Isle L.   Lac Ste. Anne

Lloydminster

(16)   Edson

Wabamun L.

EDMONTON

(16)   Vermilion

Hinton

NAT'L PARK

Saskatchewan R.

Leduc   (14)

Jasper

Pigeon L.

(2A)   Camrose

Wetaskiwin   Wainwright

N.

(13)

to Calgary

Railway's charming older Macdonald Hotel, with its great chateau-styled, peaked roofs, and Canadian Pacific Railway's modern, circular structure, the Chateau Lacombe, which stands 24 stories high on the city skyline, are in the downtown sector.

Restaurants and night clubs

Edmonton's restaurants offer a wide and varied cuisine, and, of course, steak houses feature Alberta's famous beef. The Chateau Lacombe has a revolving dining room atop the hotel, from which the view over the night-lighted city is spectacular. Visitor bureaus will provide lists of restaurants.

The capital goes in for swinging entertainment, with some 20 night clubs. Along Jasper Avenue, which cuts through the busiest part of the downtown area, and 100th Avenue, in the nine blocks between 100th and 109th Streets, 11 hotels or night clubs feature evening entertainment. All the larger hotels have both nightly revues and music for dancing.

Edmonton's "black gold"

With a population of some 450,000 in the greater Edmonton area, the capital is Alberta's largest and Canada's fourth largest city. Agriculture ranks first in the area's economy, although this is Canada's oil capital, and, after Toronto, the second largest meat processing center in the nation.

Except for the huge white oil tanks clustered southeast of town along what is called Chemical Row, and the tall, silvery spires of the refineries, there is little to suggest that Edmonton is the center of such tremendous oil reserves, yielding more than 70 per cent of the nation's oil at a rate of more than 600,000 barrels a day. Once a well is pumping oil, regulations require that the derrick come down immediately.

Interprovincial Pipeline, the longest in the world, goes through Chicago on its way to Montreal. Another, Trans-Mountain Pipeline, carries oil via the Yellowhead Pass to Vancouver and the United States Pacific Northwest.

This "black gold" was discovered in March, 1947, at Leduc, 15 miles south of town. Beside the Visitor Bureau on Highway 2 South stands the original derrick used at Leduc Number 1 Discovery Well, with a beacon and a plaque commemorating the beginning of Canada's great oil boom, which was to make Edmonton one of the nation's fastest growing cities expanding at a steady rate of about 10 per cent a year.

Places to see

You can walk to a number of interesting places near the downtown area.

Edmonton's Civic Centre, a partially completed $150 million project, includes the City Hall, the Canadian

LAWN BOWLERS play on the green turf in front of the Legislative Building in Edmonton.

PROVINCIAL MUSEUM and Archives Building houses exhibits on the natural history of the province, and on events since the arrival of the white man. Guided tours are available.

National Railway's 29-story tower, the Edmonton Art Gallery, and the spacious Centennial Library. Gleaming, functional buildings, they face Sir Winston Churchill Square, a block-square of open lawns. During Klondike Days, 25,000 guests may gather here for an outdoor barbecue, and in winter the square is flooded to create a skating rink.

A wonderful way to get oriented is from the top floor observation deck of City Hall. A cafeteria here is open to the public from 8:30 a.m. to 4 p.m. Monday through Friday, except during the noon hour, when it is reserved for civic employees.

The Art Gallery on Churchill Square hangs its paintings on broadloom-covered walls; the main gallery on the second floor houses a permanent collection of both traditional and contemporary works by Canadian artists. Traveling exhibits are hung in other large galleries.

Sculpture, a children's gallery, and a shop where you can buy art reproductions occupy the ground floor; a downstairs theater which seats 250 persons is used for special film showings.

Free, the gallery is open from 10 A.M. to 6 P.M. Monday through Saturday, and until 9 P.M. Wednesday and Thursday, and from 2 to 5 P.M. on Sunday.

The Legislative Building, a stately, high-domed, old-world edifice built between 1907 and 1912, looks out across broad, flower-bordered lawns toward the North Saskatchewan River. The Legislature's 64 members sit in session here from January until around Easter; visitors are welcome to watch the proceedings from special galleries.

Edmonton has been the capital of Alberta since the province was created in 1905. The town had been incorporated only the previous year, when it had a population of 5,000 persons.

The Legislative Building is open during the summer from 8 A.M. to 8:30 P.M. daily, with tours starting every half hour from 9 o'clock each morning. During winter, tours are offered every two hours, and the building closes at 5 P.M. On Sunday afternoons, when like other Canadian cities, Edmonton all but rolls up the sidewalks, the carillon at the Legislative Building chimes a special program at 3 o'clock.

The University of Alberta, located along the south bank of the river, has a large and beautiful campus. Its recent architecturally modern structures contrast interestingly with the earlier buildings of mellowed brick covered with traditional clinging ivy.

The university, founded in 1906 at Strathcona, which later became a part of Edmonton, is attended by about 15,000 students.

One of the most stunning structures is the black and white Student Union Building, for which the students raised the funds, and which they operate themselves. Outstanding in impressive exterior and in the quality of its facilities and instruction is the $150 million Medical Sciences complex, which, when finished, is expected to be one of the largest, as well as one of the finest, medical research centers on the North American continent. Nearly $100 million has been earmarked for expansion of other faculties of the university, and a second campus now is in the planning stage.

The Northern Alberta Institute of Technology on Princess Elizabeth Avenue also has an enrollment of approximately 12,000 students. In its 19 acres under one roof, the institute has 145 laboratories and shops.

The Jubilee Auditorium on the university campus at 87th Avenue and 114th Street is a twin to that in Calgary. It is Northern Alberta's all-purpose auditorium used for touring theatricals and concerts as well as for performances of local groups.

The Edmonton Symphony Orchestra, made up of 80 musicians, usually schedules a series of 25 concerts here during the winter season.

The Queen Elizabeth Planetarium, 111th Avenue and 136th Street in Coronation Park, was Canada's first planetarium when it was opened in 1960. Showings are given Tuesday through Saturday, from June 30 to September 1, at 3 and at 8 P.M. On Sundays and holidays, they are offered at 2, 4, and 8 P.M.; in winter, Tuesday through Sunday, they are given at 3 and 8 P.M. Children under 6 are not admitted.

Coronation Park also has football and soccer fields, baseball diamonds, a cricket pitch, tennis courts, an indoor swimming pool, and a hockey arena.

The Storyland Valley Zoo in Laurier Park is a delightful place to take children, for it has been created with much imagination. Its gateway is like the entrance to a castle. Humpty Dumpty sits on his wall, seals swim in a pond, there's a miniature barn in which to climb, two toy trains and burros to ride, and every afternoon a cow is milked.

From April 27 to October 1, Storyland is open from noon to 8 P.M. daily.

Museums

Edmonton has a number of museums to visit, several with exhibits showing the area's early days.

The Provincial Museum and Archives of Alberta, 12845 102nd Avenue, is one of the province's outstanding museums. A Confederation memorial project, this functional example of late 20th century architecture stands beside the Victorian mansion which was once the residence of Alberta's Lieutenant Governor, recently refurbished so that it may be used for official provincial gatherings. From the sweeping lawns and gardens of this former estate, you look back over the city with its winding river for one of Edmonton's loveliest views.

The natural history of the province, and the story of the white man since his arrival in Alberta in the

STORYLAND ZOO is a land of nursery rhymes. "Crooked House" at left, "Gingerbread House", right.

1700's are told here in well lighted, clearly depicted dioramas and exhibits.

Hours, from June 16 to September 16, are 9 A.M. to 9 P.M. daily except Sunday, when the museum is open from 1 to 9 P.M. Winter hours are 9 A.M. to 5 P.M. Monday through Saturday, and until 9 P.M. on Fridays; 11 A.M. to 6 P.M. on Sundays. There is no admission charge; if you want a guided tour, check in advance by calling 482-5451.

St. Albert Museum, also called the Father Lacombe Mission Museum, 5 miles north of town on Highway 2, is also free, and open from 9 A.M. to 9 P.M. Monday through Saturday, and from 1 to 9 P.M. on Sundays. The chapel-turned-museum illustrates the days of the settlers when Father Lacombe, much beloved Oblate missionary, built his church in 1861.

It was Father Lacombe who kept the Blackfoot Indians on peaceable terms with the settlers, and who persuaded the Indians that it was all right for the Canadian Pacific Railway to lay its steel tracks across their lands.

George McDougall Shrine, another church-museum that preserves mementos of Edmonton's earliest days, is just north of McDougall United Church, at 100th Avenue and 101st Street. Built by the Reverend George McDougall, a Methodist missionary who was also known for keeping the peace between Indians and settlers, it was the first structure built outside the walls of old Fort Edmonton. Free, it is open from

2 to 5 P.M. Tuesday through Saturday in summer, and noon to 1:30 P.M. on Sundays.

The Historical Exhibits Building, 101st Street at the corner of 112th Avenue, houses a different sort of collection—old-time photographs and relics that trace the very earliest recorded times of the area up to 1905, when the province was established. The museum is open from 10 A.M. to 5 P.M. daily all year; free.

The Mosque of Al Raschid, 111th Avenue and 102nd Street, with a slender minaret high on either side of the entrance, is the place of worship for the city's Muslim community. Some 200 families celebrate their Friday sabbath here. The mosque is open every day for prayers, and visitors are welcome, but remember the Muslim tradition of removing shoes before entering a mosque.

Parks

The capital has some 5,000 acres of parks, mostly along the North Saskatchewan River on both north and south banks. There's spacious Victoria Park, with its municipal golf links; Emily Murphy Park south of the river, set up for picnicking; Queen Elizabeth Park, with its popular outdoor swimming pool; and Mayfair Park, also on the south side of the river west of Groat Road, which is rather special because trout fishing in its artificial lake is reserved for anglers 16 years old and under.

Stocked with rainbow trout, the little lake occu-

DANCERS enliven downtown Edmonton during Klondike Days, commemorating gold rush of 1898.

pies a former gravel pit. Fathers can bait hooks and offer advice, but the youngsters must do the rest. The park has picnic tables, too, and in winter, the fishing pond becomes a skating rink.

Fort Edmonton Park is one of the city's typically tremendous projects now underway. On nearly 153 acres along the south shore of the river, at the southern end of Quesnel Bridge, the park when completed will portray the area's development through geological time to the present.

Already part of a frontier village and a replica of Fort Edmonton, mid-19th century Hudson's Bay trading post, have been constructed. Dioramas are planned to depict geological ages. Two Indian villages will show life among the Indians before and after the white man's arrival. Actual street scenes will recall the first lumber and grist mills, the ferry and the gold dredge of 1885, plank sidewalks, and the steamboat dock of the early years.

A hangar will be featured in the 1920's scene, for this was the era of the bush pilots who opened up the northlands, and made Edmonton the "gateway to the North" that it still is. Still another street scene will re-create the oil boom that began here in 1947.

The first Fort Edmonton was built in 1795, the name taken from a borough of London, England. Several more forts were either burned by the Indians, or moved to new locations, but all were near Edmonton's own river.

The days when the Overlanders, returning from the Cariboo gold fields, panned gold at Clover Bar in the North Saskatchewan, and the frenzied era of the 1898 Klondike Gold Rush, when miners made Edmonton their supply center on the way to the Yukon, will, of course, be part of the story as it unfolds in the new park.

Sports

Edmonton has two public golf courses, the Victoria Park course and the Riverside links at 92nd Street and Rowland Road, both 18-hole courses. Fees, which may surprise visitors, are 75 cents for 18 holes on weekdays, $1 on weekends. Half a dozen private clubs also grant visitor privileges.

Edmonton's parks abound in city-owned tennis courts, swimming pools, and trails for hiking or horseback riding.

Fishermen catch goldeye and yellow perch in the river in summer, and nearby lakes like Big Chichakoo, Star, and Cottage Lakes, all about 25 miles west of town, and Wabamun Lake, south of Highway 16 50 miles to the west, are stocked with rainbow trout.

To obtain a fishing license, look in the telephone directory for the nearest Treasury Branch. You can get both information about fishing and a fishing license there.

Winter finds 14 rinks available for that popular Canadian sport, curling, and skating rinks are all over the city. From December into March, Edmonton turns on a snow machine whenever necessary to keep its downtown ski run in full operation.

For spectators, the Edmonton Eskimos, the city's professional football club, plays at Clarke Stadium; the Oil Kings hockey team at the Edmonton Gardens; and curling bonspiels are held at the Sportex. On many a summer Sunday afternoon, you can see cricket or lacrosse being played at one of the city parks.

Thoroughbred and harness races run all summer at Northlands Park; there is auto racing at Speedway Park, and track, soccer, and English rugby contests at huge Kinsmen Field House.

Klondike Days

Every year in mid-July, Edmontonians not only recall the days of the Klondike Gold Rush, they relive them. Calling it midsummer madness, they turn back the clock to the 1890's, and for 10 gala days stage a non-stop show to which visitors get a warm welcome.

At social gatherings, or on the job, women wear the fashions of that celebrated decade, long gowns fussy with flounce and furbelow, feather boas, and wide, droopy hats, beflowered and plumed.

Men play the part as zestfully, theatrical in scarlet waistcoats, bowlers, tails, and top hats. If you want to get into the spirit of the festivities, you can rent a costume. Ask at your hotel or the visitors' bureau where to find a rental agency.

Everywhere honky-tonk pianos sound on street corners and from cafe to hotel lounge. At the Exhibition Grounds, all is carnival time, Gay 90's style.

Alberta allows gambling at agricultural fairs, and since the fair is a large part of the Klondike celebration, the Silver Slipper Gambling Saloon on the midway in Northlands Park has a large and legal crowd.

Everyday someone also wins $1,000 in gold, and at noon is rattled downtown to a bank by stagecoach, complete with outrider posse escort, to exchange it for useable currency.

All ages line the tiny stream that trickles down from the "Chilkoot Mine" at the midway to pan for gold. For 25 cents, each prospector receives a pan of sand salted with nuggets to wash in the creek. Whatever gold he finds, he may cash in at the "assay office."

Daily parades of marching bands, outdoor breakfasts in Churchill Square, barbecues in Kinsmen Field House, and a river regatta are on the schedule. On Sunday, traffic stops for the Sunday Promenade.

Other events

The Muk-Luk Mardi Gras is usually an annual event held in early February, featuring events that range

HOPEFUL PROSPECTORS of all ages wash their pans of sand as they search for gold nuggets.

CARIBOU are native to Western Canada. This one was raised at Alberta Game Farm near Edmonton.

ALBERTA GAME FARM

The Alberta Game Farm, one of the world's most unusual zoos, 14 miles east of Edmonton via Highway 14, is actually just what it is called, more farm than zoo. On his privately owned 1,500-acre preserve, famed zoologist Al Oeming both raises and displays exotic game animals from all over the globe. With a minimum of confinement, they are as free as it is possible for animals to be in a zoo.

Among his 2,500 specimens are rare creatures like the Siberian tiger, the white-tailed gnu, the waterbuck, and the wild sheep of Africa. Oeming is carrying out some highly unusual experiments. He is raising muskoxen from the tundras of the Northwest Territories, breeding wild yaks from Tibet, and watching desert and other tropical animals adjust to the cold Alberta winters. Flamingoes adapt to winter snow, Arabian camels wade knee-deep in it, and addax from the Sahara Desert grow heavy coats that withstand temperatures that may dip to 60 degrees below zero.

One of Oeming's principal goals is to reestablish rare species that have nearly become extinct like the whooping crane, the grizzly bear, and the pure wood bison, largest hoofed mammal in North America.

Grizzly bears daily stage the game farm's most exciting show. Three tiny cubs were brought in from the Swan Hills area northwest of Edmonton where man's advent, due to extensive oil production there, has tended to decimate the grizzly population. Now visitors gather round as Oeming feeds milk to one of his nearly 900-pound pets from a 3½-gallon bottle. Bottle feeding, he explains, has kept them tame.

Some of the other birds and animals may be hand fed by visitors who picnic in the wooded park near Lost Lake.

The game farm is open every day of the year from 9 A.M. to dark.

from snowshoe to snowmobile racing, dog sled competition, and elaborate ice sculptures on city streets. In March comes an indoor Rodeo of Champions; and in August the fall horse show is held.

OUT OF EDMONTON

Highways reach out from Edmonton in all directions even as the trails of Indian, fur trader, and gold seeker once did. To the east and southeast, several highways lead into the province of Saskatchewan; the most direct is the Yellowhead Route (Highway 16), which goes 156 miles to the Saskatchewan border at Lloydminster.

Along these highways are lakes and streams where the fishing is excellent for lake, brook, and rainbow trout, and for pike, perch, and walleye. Both small campgrounds and provincial parks are numerous— parks like Miquelon Lake, with its fine beaches north of Camrose, and the big park at Vermilion on Highway 16.

This same highway goes west for 228 miles to Jasper, first through farming and dairying country, then past scrubby groves of spruce that hint of the land of stunted trees and muskeg to the far north. Beyond the pulp and paper center of Hinton, quite suddenly mountains are on every side, and you are entering Jasper National Park.

Other routes from Edmonton go north, but only a few go far, for this is the beginning of that land of the midnight sun, much of it unchanged since the time of the earliest fur traders.

Highway 28, paved all the way, again with campgrounds every few miles, goes northeast to Cold Lake, known for its lake trout. Highway 46, half paved, half gravel, goes to Lac La Biche, also known for its goldeye, and for its annual August Fish Derby and Pow Wow.

North of Edmonton

Highway 63 veers north from Highway 46 to push a gravel road for 156 miles to Fort McMurray, a town of about 5,000 persons and the center of the Athabasca Oil Sands, still the largest known oil reserve in the world.

Highway 2, skirting the southern shores of Lesser Slave Lake, runs north to Peace River, then bends southwest to Grand Prairie, 285 miles northwest of the capital. Then it crosses the British Columbia border to Dawson Creek, takeoff point for the long road to Alaska.

From Grimshaw, 16 miles west of Peace River, the Mackenzie Highway pushes on and on by gravel road into the north, all the way to Yellowknife on the northern shores of Great Slave Lake in the Northwest Territories.

Only unimproved roads, and few of those, trail into

MONUMENT in Peace River to 12-Foot Davis, who made a fortune.

ONLY SUSPENSION BRIDGE in the province spans the Peace River near Dunvegan on Highway 2 near the British Columbia border.

the myriad lakes of this northern region (fishermen and hunters fly into them by charter plane from Edmonton).

The Peace River Valley

Some of Canada's finest farming land is in the Peace River Valley. This great stream, which seems always to have been called the Peace, even in Indian folklore, begins in British Columbia as the Finlay and the Parsnip Rivers. Southeast of Fort Saint John, it enters Alberta, swings in wide arcs through the town of Peace River, goes northeast through Fort Vermilion, where a fur trading post was built by the North West Company in 1798, and across vast Wood Buffalo National Park. The river flows for 1,000 miles through the province before reaching Lake Athabasca, the Slave and the Mackenzie Rivers, and ultimately the Arctic Ocean.

Dinosaurs roamed this Peace River region, their tracks having been discovered in the river canyon. The stream was the water route for the earliest explorers, among them Sir Alexander Mackenzie, who traveled it by canoe on his expedition across to the Pacific Ocean in 1792.

Moose hunting

Most of this wide area north of 54° north latitude is set aside as Big Game Zone 1, in which non-residents may hunt moose. An alien license entitles the holder to kill one moose of either sex in this region during the autumn-winter season.

Peace River loop

To sample the Peace River country, try a loop trip on Highway 2A from Valleyview through Peace River to Grande Prairie (212 miles of paved road), or vice versa. Provincial parks like Winagami Lake, southeast of Donnelly, and Lac Cardinal, 4 miles northwest of Grimshaw, offer tent and trailer parking sites, swimming, boating, and fishing, particularly for northern pike.

At Peace River, where Mackenzie built a trading post, see the monument of "12-Foot Davis," the miner who became legend when, in crowded Barkerville during the Cariboo gold rush, he noticed that two gold claims exceeded the legal limit by 12 feet. He staked the 12 feet, and took some $15,000 in gold from the claim.

At Saskatoon Island Provincial Park, 15 miles west of Grand Prairie, you may be able to see the nesting grounds of the rare trumpeter swan.

Lesser Slave Lake Provincial Park, 4 miles north of the town of Slave Lake on Highway 2, has three large campgrounds in the park's 28 square miles. This is one of Alberta's largest lakes—55 miles long—with wide, white sandy beaches, a great place for swimming, boating, and fishing.

Index

PHOTOGRAPHERS

ALBERTA GOVERNMENT: pages 72, 81 (top), 84 (top), 85, 90, 95. MIMI BELL: pages 6, 7 (left), 12, 14 (right), 15, 17, 21, 22 (top left, bottom left, bottom right), 24 (left), 25, 26 (right), 27, 33, 35, 43 (bottom), 61 (right), 62, 66 (right), 75, 77, 79, 84 (bottom), 89, 93. BRITISH COLUMBIA GOVERNMENT: pages 11, 19 (right), 26 (left), 31, 36, 38 (right), 39, 45 (left), 46, 49, 51 (bottom), 54, 55, 67. CALGARY TOURIST AND CONVENTION ASSOCIATION: page 81 (bottom). CALGARY WHITE HATTERS: page 71. CANADIAN GOVERNMENT: pages 14 (left), 22 (top right), 24 (right), 45 (right), 64, 66 (left), 82 (right), 83. CITY OF EDMONTON: pages 87, 92. CITY OF PRINCE RUPERT: page 51 (top). FRANCES COLEBERD: pages 52 (top), 73. DOLLY CONNELLY: pages 53, 61 (left). RICH-ARD DAWSON: page 13. JACK DE LORME PHOTOGRAPHY LTD.: page 82 (left). CHUCK DIVEN: page 29. EDMONTON JOURNAL: page 91. BRUNO ENGLER: page 63. CLIFFORD A. FENNER: page 28 (left). GRAPHIC INDUSTRIES LTD.: page 28 (right). GREATER VANCOUVER VISITORS AND CONVENTION BUREAU: page 23. KELOWNA CHAMBER OF COMMERCE: page 37. DON NORMARK: pages 8, 22 (bottom center), 38 (left), 44. PETRIGO OF CANADA: page 80. PETE REDPATH: page 41. HARRY ROWED: pages 7 (right), 56, 59, 65, 67 (left), 68, 69, 70. GEORGE SCHOFIELD: page 94. BOB AND IRA SPRING: pages 19 (left), 43 (top). JOE VAN WORMER: page 52 (bottom). ELTON WELKE: pages 18, 47.